PORTILLO'S
HIDDEN
HISTORY
OF
BRITAIN

MICHAEL PORTILLO

Michael O'Mara Books Limited

This paperback edition first published in 2019

First published in Great Britain in 2018 by
Michael O'Mara Books Limited
9 Lion Yard
Tremadoc Road
London SW4 7NQ

A CIP catalogue record for this book is available from the British Library.

Papers used by Michael O'Mara Books Limited are natural, recyclable products made from wood grown in sustainable forests. The manufacturing processes conform to the environmental regulations of the country of origin.

ISBN: 978-1-78929-144-5 in paperback print format
ISBN: 978-1-78929-064-6 in hardback print format
ISBN: 978-1-78929-049-3 in ebook format
ISBN: 978-1-78929-095-0 in audio format

1 2 3 4 5 6 7 8 9 10

Editorial Consultant: Nigel Richardson
Cover design by Patrick Knowles
Designed and typeset by K.DESIGN, Winscombe, Somerset
Printed and bound by CPI Group (UK) Ltd, Croydon, CR0 4YY

www.mombooks.com

Contents

Acknowledgements

The author would like to thank:

Ben Frow, Craig Morris VP, Guy Davies and the team at Channel 5; Jazz Gowans, CEO at Transparent Television, Ruairi Fallon, Executive Producer at Transparent Television, Victoria Gardner Head of Development at Transparent Television, Emma Linstead Archive Producer Transparent Television and the team at Transparent Television; Lou Plank and the team at Plank PR; The Royal London Hospital Museum; Richard Meunier, Archivist; Dr Adrian Thomas; Dr Alastair Mulcahy; Barts Health NHS Trust; Tower Hamlets Council; National Trust, Orford; Fred Davis; Ben Gunn; Ministry of Defence; Gordon and Anne Lewis; Jane Paget; Beth Junor; David Johnson; Bradford Council; Bradford Live; Mark Nicholson; Paul Berriff; Dr Andrew Bamji; Diana Cowell; Doug Vince; Prof John Allen; Allied London; Bob Bonner and Greater

Manchester Fire Service Museum; All the men and women who worked at London Road Fire Station and helped us with the programme; XM655 Maintenance and Preservation Society at Wellesbourne Airfield; The University of Cambridge; Brighton West Pier Trust; Southern Water; Jo Berry; Saltdean Lido Community Interest Company.

The publishers would like to thank:

Stuart Cooper; Nigel Richardson; All the team at Transparent Television; Helen Cumberbatch; Nicki Crossley; Kay Hayden.

Introduction

Scattered across Britain there are many extraordinary buildings and structures that have outlived their original purpose. There they lie, in the back streets of provincial towns, on remote stretches of coast, in the centres of cities: abandoned, boarded up, mysterious. Each hides a unique narrative, of personal endeavour or heartbreak, of momentous events that shaped the nation. In this book, and in the television series from which it sprang, I explore twelve such sites, shining a light into their cobwebbed corners to reveal a hidden history of modern Britain.

I was trained as a historian at Cambridge University and since I left politics and turned to broadcasting some twenty years ago, I have made a number of television and radio programmes with historical themes. In them, I have found myself being drawn again and again to buildings – because they featured in a historical event, or could illuminate some aspect of history, or simply because I found them arresting to look at. Buildings that have caught my eye and suited my purpose range from the Royal Crescent in Bath to the Dome of the Rock in Jerusalem. But, however splendid, they were incidental to my theme of the moment.

In *Portillo's Hidden History of Britain* I wished to switch that perspective around, to focus on my fascination with buildings – their beauty, their purpose, the stories hidden in their walls. The way into a particular subject is a vital consideration for the popular historian. In a radio series I made entitled *Things We Forgot to Remember*, I revisited great moments in history that are largely misremembered in the popular retelling, such as 'Magna Carta' and 'Jesse Owens and the Nazi Olympics'. In my television travels by train, a focus has been on how the railways changed societies. The idea of *Portillo's Hidden History of Britain* is to put a building (or structure – I made the definition loose enough to include obvious 'non-buildings' such as a submarine) centre stage and invite it to 'speak' to us.

Over the course of two television series I have explored some remarkable sites, from the south coast to Yorkshire and East Anglia to the West Country. In most cases they were derelict and abandoned, on the point of changing into something else. This made my intervention particularly opportune: I got in at the eleventh hour, before much of the fabric of the original building was destroyed or changed beyond recognition. From prison to sewer, from bunker to pier, they have helped me understand some of the ways in which modern Britain has developed.

In the course of filming, I accumulated a wealth of material – personal testimonies, documents, letters, photographs – which was crying out for more detailed examination and exposure. The book you are holding is the result. It has allowed me the time and scope to elaborate on important themes and place them in context. Whether on screen or page, the structures I explored became 'witnesses' or 'documents' in their own right, to be listened to and interpreted. Some were more or less intact and therefore relatively straightforward to make sense of. Shepton Mallet prison, in Somerset, for example, looked practically the same as on the day it closed in 2013, which is not to say that the stories it revealed weren't eye-popping. On the other hand, the West Pier at Brighton barely exists, is a mere and diminishing skeleton that offers next to no clues about what happened there. Yet, in the end, its testament was just as powerful.

By the same token some buildings confounded expectations. When I visited Cambridge Military Hospital in Aldershot I had already dissected the rich and significant history of the Royal London Hospital in London's East End. I had expected the military hospital's background to be comparable, one of pioneering medical work with an emphasis, in this case, on the peculiar challenges posed by battle injuries. Only up to a point was this true. Beyond, I discovered a story that teeters on the edge of the credible.

I found the building-based approach genuinely liberating. Sleuthing around the dusty corners of atmospheric old places gave full rein to my sense of curiosity, while drawing on a natural scepticism that I developed as a history undergraduate. It's important that historians ask themselves, 'How do I know this, who told me, how did it pass down through the years or the generations, what is the foundation for this piece of knowledge?' For a politician to be overburdened with scepticism, by the way, is not necessarily a good thing: too often you are required to express a remarkable degree of enthusiasm for a new policy when your experience tells you that it's very unlikely to be the panacea that your party claims. This is why, in the end, broadcasting now suits me.

I should point out, however, that I am no David Starkey or Simon Schama. I am not an academic and nor have I confined my interest to a particular era or aspect of history. I am a generalist who wishes to take the reader or viewer along with me on my explorations. And sometimes my initial instincts are wrong, or I am simply baffled by what I find. This is why, for the television series and book of *Portillo's Hidden History of Britain*, I arranged to meet people along the way who know more about each structure than I can ever know. In this way the project has been as much a journey of discovery for me as I believe it will be for you.

Some of these witnesses were experts, on the ballistics of nuclear bombs, for example. Many were just ordinary people who were caught up in extraordinary events – such as the college leaver from Lancashire pitched into the cloak-and-dagger world of the Cold War. One witness, with an incredible life story to tell, made more of an impression on me than just about anyone I have interviewed in my broadcasting career. All offered a perspective that was far more vivid than simply looking at a diagram or reading a passage in a book. I am happy to acknowledge that in some cases this approach introduced a certain bias to my recording of history. Because I was insistent on including, where possible, eyewitness accounts, I tended to concentrate on events that people are still alive to remember – which means, effectively, from the 1920s onwards (the oldest person I interviewed was 102).

This is partly why the Second World War pops up in some surprising contexts. Nevertheless, that epic conflict has been central to the shaping of modern Britain – our politics, our economy, our place in the world, our very character. And it is modern Britain, in the end, that is the subject of this book. In it, I attempt to illustrate how we have developed as a nation in certain key areas, which I divide into four sections. These are 'Crime and Emergency' which looks at prisons and the work of firefighters and first responders; 'Life and Death', on the evolution of healthcare and much more; 'Defence of the Realm', which examines top-secret installations and dramatizes the moment when the world stood on the brink of nuclear annihilation; and 'People's Pleasure Domes', about, essentially, how we entertain and distract ourselves.

Throughout I have tried to keep the building – the place itself – in the front of the picture. Many, such as the military hospital in Aldershot, deserve to be there simply as examples of bold, imposing design. The bizarre structures scattered across the shingle spit of Orford Ness, on the other hand, are by no stretch of the imagination beautiful. But they are haunting, puzzling, and they contribute to a landscape as otherworldly as any in Britain. Everywhere I visited was built with care and skill for a purpose that commands respect – and that applies most particularly to the site that represents hidden Britain in a literal sense: the sewers beneath Brighton.

As already mentioned, several of the buildings were about to be rebuilt and it was crucial that I gained access when I did. Hearteningly, one of them, the New Victoria Cinema in Bradford, is being returned to its original purpose as a cinema and entertainment centre. But most are being 'repurposed', most commonly as blocks of flats. This is not necessarily a fate I would have wished on them but it is preferable, in my opinion, to having them razed to the ground and a car park or shopping centre put in their place.

I am sufficiently pragmatic to realize that however beautiful or remarkable a building may be, you can't simply stick it in the deep freeze when it has outlived its usefulness. But before the men in hard hats move in you *can* cup your ear close and listen to what it has to say. And that is what I have attempted here. If walls could speak, these are some of the stories they would tell.

PART I

Crime and Emergency

I am happy to declare myself a supporter of authority. I am a great admirer of people who dedicate their lives to upholding the power and obligations of the state in terms of criminal justice, from Home Secretaries to gaolers and from judges to police officers. But equally, I am a natural sceptic and perfectly willing to believe that the state makes errors. In the case of one man I met while researching this section, the errors were multiple and egregious. His story raised an important, uncomfortable question. What is prison *for*?

Ben Gunn is a former inmate at Shepton Mallet prison, which was the oldest in Britain when it closed in 2013. He served nearly half a lifetime behind bars. He was not an innocent man. The crime that sent him to jail was murder, the worst a person can commit, but that, in the end, doesn't seem to have been the principal reason for keeping him banged up – most convicted murderers serve less time than he did. No, his 'error' was that he didn't fit into the prison system. What a fantastic paradox, that because he didn't fit into the system he was forced to remain within it for more than thirty years.

It was to understand something of that 'system' that I had gone to Shepton Mallet. What is it like for those who, by wickedness, foolishness or sheer bad luck, end up inside? What does it feel like when that cell door bangs closed and you are left with nothing but the bare physical essentials and endless tracts of time in which to reflect on the actions that brought you there? Prisons have been around for as long as human beings have lived in organized societies, under agreed codes of law and behaviour. Shepton Mallet's lifespan as a working prison covers hundreds of years and its history illuminates our changing attitudes to crime and punishment.

I didn't feel entirely comfortable about entering Shepton's forbidding precincts, for reasons I explain in the chapter, but my reluctance was as nothing compared to Ben's. His first words to me were: 'It's not a happy place.' And during the few hours he spent back behind the walls that had deprived him of liberty and meaningful life for so long, he often struggled to contain his emotions and fear.

From everything he told me it seems he took his punishment on the chin. He also made the most of his time, gaining two degrees. But he has struggled to see a wider purpose for incarceration. 'You can't have punishment and rehabilitation simultaneously,' he told me. 'You can't punch someone in the mouth and give them a Band-Aid.' As for deterrence, Shepton Mallet has its own cautionary tale. The Kray twins, two of the most notorious characters in British criminal history, served time there when it was a military 'glasshouse'. They were young at the time, they still had the chance to turn their lives around. Instead, prison seems to have attached rocket boosters to their nascent criminality. It is Ben's opinion that, in the end, the prison system is not about prisoners at all, but rather 'for making everybody else feel better'.

In my broadcasting career I have conducted a lot of interviews with remarkable people but I rate this encounter at Shepton Mallet as the most compelling and thought-provoking. Nevertheless, it was a relief to get prison out of my hair and travel north to Manchester to meet a body of people for whom my respect is boundless. These are the men and women of the fire service, whose role is to rescue us from fire, car crashes, natural disasters and the like – to rush towards danger as everyone else runs away. The response of the fire brigade to the terrible conflagration at Grenfell Tower in west London in June 2017 was a reminder, if any were needed, of the bravery and commitment of this rare breed of public servant.

My plan was to tell the story of these Manchester firefighters through the station in which they served. What I hadn't bargained on was the scale and ambition of that building, which is situated in London Road near Manchester Piccadilly railway station. Its design, in fact, is similar to Shepton Mallet prison, for they share a striking feature. Each, for contrasting reasons, is a kind of citadel, built around a central courtyard and presenting high walls to the world. It was from here that appliances rattled out, bells clanging, to douse the flames of incendiary bombs dropped by the Luftwaffe in the Second Word War. Thirty Manchester firemen were killed in the war and it was intensely moving to be shown a fire-damaged relic of one of the worst infernos, in which two men from the London Road station lost their lives.

People have been dousing fires for even longer than they have been locking each other up in prisons. But fighting fires occurred on an ad hoc basis and well into the Middle Ages it was not unusual for entire towns of timber-framed buildings to be razed by fire, with no organized body responsible for, or equal to, fire prevention on such a scale. This situation began to change following the Great Fire of London in 1666 and the first municipal fire brigade in Britain was founded in Edinburgh in 1824. The London Road Fire Station, which closed in 1986, offered a glorious window into the evolution of firefighting in the twentieth century and represented, down to its very design, an Edwardian ideal of service to the community.

For what I hadn't realized, until I started my investigations there, was that London Road was a residential station. Not only did the firefighters work alongside each other on dangerous call-outs but they lived, literally, on top of each other. It was a real pleasure to meet men who had grown up here and listen to them reminiscing so enthusiastically about their childhoods within those high walls. It was, effectively, a giant adventure playground – the biggest dare of all being to climb 100 feet to the top of the hose tower when all the crews were out and they had forgotten to lock the tower door.

It was a place very much *of* Manchester, right in the heart of the city, yet apart from it by virtue of the enclosing walls. It wasn't until I talked to a firefighter who had attended the Moss Side Riots of 1981, that I fully understood this relationship with the community. He had been astonished to see bricks being hurled at his appliance as he and his colleagues attempted to contain the fire and damage around them. It was a reminder that a firefighter must remain apart and impartial, whatever the circumstances or provocation.

The firefighters of the London Road station stood side by side, in work and play. It was an honour to stand with them, however briefly. It may seem like a small point but it was also instructive to wear the uniform and to operate a fire hose, feel the colossal physical power of it and understand the seriousness of its purpose. The tools of my trade are laptop, pen and paper. However fraught a day I am having, I am not expected to save the lives of others and risk mine in the process.

Shepton Mallet Prison, Somerset

The sedate Somerset market town of Shepton Mallet is probably best known for being the nearest place of any size to the site of the popular Glastonbury music festival. But lying to the east of the high street is a complex of stone buildings whose purpose was altogether less joyous. As I approached it on foot, the first thing that struck me – struck the fear of God into me, if I'm honest – was its perimeter wall of grey limestone whose height I could only guess at (which I later discovered to be at least 35 feet). This forms the outer rampart of Shepton Mallet prison. I was feeling the force field of a place that for centuries was a byword for human misery.

When it closed in 2013, after nearly 400 years in continuous use, Shepton Mallet had been the oldest working gaol in Britain. Within its walls some terrible things have happened. Hard labour and poor diet broke the toughest of men, military prisoners were hanged and shot with scant regard for legal process, and there was even, at one point, a human treadmill – a grim motif of hopelessness. But, as I was about to find out, the human spirit also found ways of soaring free of its dark precincts and barred windows.

When I travelled down to Somerset, plans were in the pipeline to turn former HMP Shepton Mallet into luxury apartments. Soon it will become a hard-hat site as the cramped cells are knocked together to produce spacious living areas and the old yards are landscaped with greenery. In the process much historical evidence will inevitably be lost or obscured. Thankfully the developers had granted me special access before so much as a brick of the old prison had been touched.

The freedom to explore its corners and secrets provided me with a rare opportunity to reveal the fascinating history of this particular gaol. But there was a wider context, expressed in Nelson Mandela's dictum that 'no one truly knows a nation until one has been inside its gaols'. Shepton Mallet may have been one of the smallest gaols in the country – accommodating only 189 prisoners when it was decommissioned – but its story reflects the way in which Britain has punished its criminals over the centuries.

Full disclosure at this point: I have a recurring nightmare. I'm in prison, banged up in a tiny cell, and I have no idea by what miscalculation or misdemeanour I ended up there. I have visited jails briefly a few times to see friends – I *was* an MP, after all – but the idea of being in one still fills me with anxiety.

Exploring the cheerless reaches of Shepton Mallet, then, was not going to be easy. Would the experience of spending time in a place of incarceration, of getting to understand something of the reality of human lives deprived of freedom, help me to sleep easier – or intensify the nightmare?

First impressions were not promising. I wasn't sure whether I was imagining it but, standing in the central courtyard looking up at the rows of cell windows, I fancied there was still a stench of 'bird' about the place, a mingled aroma of slop buckets, tobacco and despair. The old signage was still there: 'No inmates allowed in yard unless under escort' (will they keep these signs in the new residential development, to add a 'heritage' flavour?). The layout was classic cell-block architecture dating from the late eighteenth century. To the north was the entrance and administration block. On the other three sides and rising to three storeys, A, B and D Wings, with C Wing lying to the south.

All this I could take in reasonably calmly. Going into one of the wings was a different matter. Inside, galleried walkways were built around a central atrium, with lines of cells set back on the walkways. Taking a deep breath I climbed the stairs to a gallery and stepped into a cell. Inside there was a bed frame, a lavatory bowl and a washbasin. I rough-measured its extent: ten paces by five. I banged the door closed and immediately wondered how long I could resist the temptation to fling it open again. A couple of minutes was all I managed. Of course I was free to do this. What would it have been like to have had that freedom taken away? To have been locked up here for most of the waking day?

I couldn't answer such a question. Prisons are by definition closed environments. They do not surrender their secrets easily. And unless you have experienced life inside a prison first-hand you cannot begin to understand what it must be like. To help me in my task of uncovering the darker truths of Shepton Mallet I had arranged to meet on site a number of experts and witnesses to prison life who knew the reality of being incarcerated at Her Majesty's pleasure. One of them had served a life sentence, much of it here at Shepton Mallet. His name was John Gunn (known to all and sundry as 'Ben') and he had lived in a prison cell for thirty-two years.

It had been a delicate negotiation, persuading him to come back to a place that held such terrible memories and I was a little apprehensive about meeting him face-to-face. He was, by all accounts, a thoughtful, articulate person, but because our lives had taken such divergent paths I wondered if we would find any common ground. We met in the shadow of that perimeter wall. The nickname Ben, incidentally, originated in his prison days when he grew a beard so long and shaggy that somebody likened him to the character Ben Gunn in Robert Louis Stevenson's classic adventure novel *Treasure Island*. He was clean-shaven now, wore a fedora and cut a self-possessed figure. But he admitted to feeling overwhelmed on his return to the institution that had deprived him of freedom for so long.

'It's not a happy place,' was the first thing he said to me.

'If you live here you try to make it work, create some sort of meaning in a meaningless environment. But it's a place of pain. We were all murderers, rapists, the most horrible people.' Shepton Mallet, in Ben's time, was for category C life prisoners. The 'C' meant they were 'unlikely to try to escape', but 'life' indicated they were guilty of the most serious crimes. Ben's crime was as serious as it gets: 'Murder,' he confirmed, adding, 'I had a fight with a mate of mine. He got grievously injured, died a couple of days later. I pleaded guilty. Off I went to prison for life.'

This was another thing I had to confront – my instinctive revulsion at meeting a person who had committed the ultimate taboo and taken a human life. But from the outset I found it hard to square my preconception of a murderer with the measured man who stood in front of me. The idea had been for Ben to take me to his old cell where he would fill me in on the background to his case and share some insights into his personal experience of serving time for more than three decades. But as we walked towards his former wing he became visibly distressed. 'People lived here but people also died here,' he said. 'A couple of suicides. Friends of mine.' We agreed that I should leave him while he gathered his thoughts and feelings. When we resumed our conversation later in the day he would reveal an astonishing side to his story that made me see him in a completely new light.

For now, I continued my exploration of the prison. Behind the wall of an office in the old gatehouse, workmen had recently discovered a cell dating from the prison's seventeenth-century origins as a 'house of correction'. I stooped to clamber through the hole in the outer wall and found myself in a claustrophobic stone chamber where I fought to suppress a feeling of rising panic. The house of correction was effectively a human dustbin where minor criminals, indigents and vagrants were confined and set to work with the aim of 'correcting' their behaviour. Men, women and children were all thrown together in a cell like this, in conditions that, even by the standards of the day, were appalling.

In the early 1770s the prison reformer John Howard (whose name was later adopted by the Howard League for Penal Reform) inspected Shepton Mallet and may well have entered this very cell. His description of 'emaciated, dejected' inmates 'expiring on the floors, in loathsome cells of pestilential fevers and the confluent smallpox' was entirely imaginable to me as I stood there with sweat breaking out on my neck. I couldn't wait to get out and stand again in the fresh air, looking up at what Oscar Wilde, in *The Ballad of Reading Gaol*, called 'that little tent of blue/Which prisoners call the sky'.

Partly as a result of Howard's criticism the prison was enlarged and improved in the eighteenth and nineteenth centuries. In 1823 a treadwheel was installed, worked by prisoners sentenced to hard labour, which was used to grind corn in a mill on the other side of the prison wall until 1890. The treadwheel was dismantled and the mill knocked down long ago, but a history of the prison, compiled by a former Shepton

Mallet prison officer and librarian, Francis Disney, contains a list of those sentenced to hard labour who would have been put to work on the treadwheel. It includes a reference to sixteen-year-old John Head in 1842. His crime? Stealing two cows' tails.

This may seem a far cry from the more enlightened penal philosophy of the modern era, with its emphasis on rehabilitation and education (however patchily provided), but the regime at Shepton Mallet more than a century later wasn't exactly a vicar's tea party either. It was in the days when the prison served as a 'glasshouse' – a military prison and detention centre – and the toughness of its inmates was matched only by the brutality of a system designed to keep them in check.

The most notorious of those inmates were the Kray twins, whose murderous proclivities dominated the narrative of crime in post-war Britain. They have generated a veritable cottage industry of books, films and articles – much of it having only a passing acquaintance to the truth. So, to find out what really happened to them at Shepton Mallet and the influence it had on their subsequent lives, I turned to a journalist and author who actually knew them. Readers of a certain age will remember Fred Dinenage as a children's television presenter and a newsreader, but Fred also worked with the Kray twins on their autobiographies. When we met at Shepton Mallet he offered to take me to the one place in the gaol of which the Krays had fond memories, explaining on the way that 'they came here a couple of young, tough tearaways and nine months later they left as fully accomplished gangsters'.

In 1952 Ronnie and Reggie Kray were a couple of jack-the-lads from London's East End with a few professional boxing fights under their belts and several convictions for violence. National Service, the conscription of young men between the ages of seventeen and twenty-one, was made compulsory in 1949, but when the nineteen-year-old Krays received their call-up papers for the Royal Fusiliers they decided that army life was an irksome distraction they could do without. So they went on the run, were apprehended and detained several times (assaulting several policemen and soldiers along the way) and were eventually sentenced to nine months in the glasshouse at Shepton Mallet, followed by a dishonourable discharge.

'Within these walls they met some very interesting characters,' Fred told me. The Krays' future life of crime, violence and murder was not preordained, even if it would be hard to imagine them settling down in Bethnal Green as pillars of the local Rotary Club. But the company they kept in the Shepton Mallet glasshouse surely had a huge influence on the way they turned out, for their fellow inmates included violent young criminals from the seamier sides of cities throughout Britain.

Among them was the south London gangster and torture specialist Charlie Richardson, whose National Service had been cut short by a court martial for assaulting an army medical officer. The regime at Shepton Mallet was so harsh, said Fred, that even apprentice hard men like Richardson and the Krays were intimidated by it. But Ronnie found light relief in the unlikeliest of places.

Fred led me into a two-storey, red-brick building attached to the south side of the main block and said with macabre jocularity, 'Welcome, Michael, to the topping shed!' We were standing in the chamber that housed the gallows on which wartime prisoners were executed by hanging. It was built during the Second World War, when the US military ran the prison – a period I shall come on to presently. After the war the execution chamber was converted into offices and the gallows boarded up. But everyone knew it was there. Fred indicated some loose floorboards in the centre of the room on the first floor and invited me to lift them up. Beneath was a piece of chilling archaeology – the square aperture where the trapdoor of the gallows had been.

'The Kray brothers were absolutely fascinated by this – particularly Ron, who had a macabre sense of humour,' explained Fred. 'He thought how nice it would be to pretend to be hanged here. And they persuaded a friendly officer, one "Doc" Holliday, to allow them in ... Noose around his neck. Dropped him – with Ronnie of course holding on very tight [to the rope] so he didn't hang himself. He thought that was very funny, in fact he said to me it was the only light moment of their whole time here.'

Now I'm no criminal psychiatrist, but the fact that Ronnie Kray's idea of respite from the brutality of the glasshouse regime was to play-act his own death by hanging is hardly indicative of a well-adjusted human being. The Krays were barely into their twenties at this point but the die was cast. Within a short time

31

of their release from Shepton Mallet the twins had bought the Regal Billiard Hall on the Mile End Road in London's East End and embarked on a life of crime based on protection rackets and violent intimidation. It's hard to avoid the conclusion that in the immediate post-war years the Shepton Mallet glasshouse was effectively a finishing school for hoodlums.

A decade earlier the prison had fulfilled a very different and totally unexpected role. My next interviewee, local historian Fred Davis, was waiting for me in C Wing with a black-and-white photograph that looked frankly uninteresting on initial inspection. It showed two men apparently sorting through files. But when Fred said matter-of-factly that 'here we've got Mr Johnson and another archivist handling the Domesday Book' and then confirmed that the photograph was taken here in Shepton Mallet prison, I was flabbergasted. It turns out that as well as functioning as a detention centre for the American military, the prison had become a place of safekeeping for some of Britain's most important national documents that dated back over 1,000 years. The archivist in charge of them, Harold Johnson, had moved his wife and family here during the war and Fred had subsequently received the photographs he was now showing me from Mrs Johnson.

We were joined on C Wing by the historian Richard Taylor, who has written a book on this extraordinary and, at the time, highly classified episode. 'It was fairly clear from May 1939 that war was a very real possibility,' he said. 'The documents from the National Archives were all in the Public Record Office in

Chancery Lane in London. A single bomb could have destroyed the lot of them.' The decision was taken to remove them to secure facilities in the regions. Among them was Belvoir Castle in Leicestershire. But Shepton Mallet was reserved for the most precious material.

'Three hundred tons of documents were brought to Shepton Mallet prison,' said Richard. 'It's in the middle of nowhere, a long way from any likely German bombs. They had to clear thirty miles of shelf space. They loaded them up on trucks which were so heavy that they all kept breaking down. And then they filled the cells.' The former women's prison, now C Wing, was given over to box upon box of letters, official papers, charters, deeds and notes pertaining to the most significant figures and events in our nation's history.

They included the Little and Great Domesday Books of 1086, the logbooks of HMS *Victory*, dispatches from the Battle of Waterloo in 1815 and that notorious piece of paper waved by Neville Chamberlain when he returned from meeting Adolf Hitler in 1938 to declare 'Peace for our time'. They were, as Richard said, 'more than just records, they were part of what makes us in Britain British'. And the most valuable and iconic was undoubtedly the document known as Magna Carta.

Richard took Fred and me to the cell where Magna Carta was stored and we stood there in a kind of reverent silence. 'I think a certain magic gets left behind when you know a great person has been in a particular place, and that's also true of a great document,' he said. Drawn up in the reign of King John in 1215, Magna Carta introduced the idea of a right to a fair trial and no detention without due process. The hefty tome stored here (one of four extant copies) was an early blueprint of human liberty and as such embodied some of the very values we were fighting the war to defend.

Magna Carta and the rest of the priceless hoard were not simply dumped here and locked in for the duration, like some incorrigible lifer. They were supervised by Harold Johnson, whose wife Fred knew. 'There are some wonderful stories about his family,' said Richard. 'They set up a little swing for his daughter. His son had a model train set and ran the railway track around the gallery. They made, by all accounts, quite a cosy little home here.'

From 1942 the Johnsons shared their 'cosy little home' with 'the useless dregs of the great American Army that had come to the United Kingdom from across the sea'. The quote is from *The Dirty Dozen*, the 1965 novel by E. M. Nathanson that inspired the 1967 film of the same name starring Lee Marvin and Charles Bronson. The 'dozen' men are a bunch of renegade American soldiers awaiting execution or lengthy prison sentences, who are recruited for a presumed suicide mission behind enemy lines. Nathanson called the fictional military prison where these ne'er-do-wells languish 'Marston-Tyne', located it in Somerset and based it on Shepton Mallet, which for the latter half of the Second World War served as a guardhouse and disciplinary centre for the US Army.

The United States had formally entered the war against Nazi Germany in December 1941. In January 1942 American servicemen and equipment began arriving in the UK as part of a military build-up that eventually brought more than 1.5 million US soldiers and airmen to these shores. Under the USA (Visiting Forces) Act of 1942 they were subject to American military justice during their stay and one of the principal centres for the administration of that justice was Shepton Mallet gaol.

It was handed over to the US military in 1942 and staffed by American personnel until the end of the war. Eighteen US soldiers were executed here – nine for murder, six for rape and three for both offences. And of the eighteen, ten were black and three Hispanic – disturbing figures when one considers that nine out of ten US soldiers were white. But it's the story of an African-American serviceman who *escaped* execution that I was particularly interested in, for his case served to highlight wider issues of class and race which still reverberate today.

On 25 May 1944, as Allied forces across the south of England geared up for D-Day (on 6 June), thirty-year-old Private Leroy Henry, a truck driver from St Louis, Missouri, appeared before a court martial at a US Army Camp in Wiltshire. The charge was that on 5 May he had raped a thirty-three-year-old woman in the village of Combe Down near Bath. According to the alleged victim and her husband, both of whom gave evidence at the court martial, the couple were in bed, asleep, on the night in question when the accused had knocked on the door and woken them up.

In their version of events the American had said he was lost and asked for directions to Bristol. The woman put a coat on over her nightdress and walked down the road with him to point the way. When they were some distance from the house he pulled a knife on her and ordered her to climb over a wall into a field, where he raped her. Henry pleaded not guilty, claiming that he had arranged to visit the woman for sex and that after they had had sex they had fallen out over the fee – she demanded £2, but he was only prepared to pay £1, which was the amount they had agreed on two previous occasions.

The prosecution produced a signed confession, which Henry claimed he had not read and had signed only after being beaten by the military police. Despite the lack of corroborating evidence and the woman's improbable explanation for her behaviour in following a complete stranger out into the night, the jury of eight officers – seven white and one black – found him guilty. Henry was sentenced to death by hanging and the sentence was to be carried out at Shepton Mallet prison.

At this point it looked as though Private Henry would be just a footnote in history – another name to add to the list of military prisoners executed at Shepton Mallet after hasty trials of dubious rigour. But as he awaited his fate in one of the condemned cells in that red-brick chamber, a grass-roots campaign for his release was organized, which has much in common with the social-media campaigns of the present age.

Many people in Bath who read the details of the court martial were disturbed by the guilty verdict. They knew the supposed victim worked as a part-time prostitute, and some of the residents of Combe Down had seen the soldier and the woman drinking together in a local pub. People were, furthermore, well disposed towards African-American servicemen, who had travelled far from home to defend our freedoms, and indignant at the blatantly discriminatory treatment to which they were often subjected – for example, being hauled out of English pubs and dance halls by 'snowdrops' (US military police) enforcing the same 'Jim Crow' segregation laws that then prevailed in the southern states of America.

Cecil King, the publisher of the *Daily Mirror*, observed the situation shrewdly in an entry in his personal war diary, written the day after the Henry verdict: 'The feeling is fairly common that Negroes are nicer and better behaved than the ordinary Yank. So there is some indignation when Negro soldiers are condemned to death for raping English girls. In the most recent case [of Leroy Henry] the evidence would most certainly have resulted in an acquittal in an English court. In the far more numerous cases of rape or murder by white American soldiers, the punishment, if any, is of a wholly different order of severity.'

A local baker and his daughter started a petition urging a review of Private Henry's conviction. It was circulated in the Bath area and printed in the local paper, gathering 33,000 signatures in a short space of time. The story received widespread coverage in Britain, and in New York the campaigning organization known as the National Association for the Advancement of Colored Peoples (NAACP) took up the soldier's cause. On

3 June 1944, the NAACP sent a telegram to General Dwight D. Eisenhower, the most senior figure in the US Army and Supreme Commander of the Allied Expeditionary Forces for Operation Overlord, asking him to order a stay of execution for Henry and a review of his case.

Eisenhower, despite having the small matter of the invasion of occupied Europe on his plate, did more than that. On 17 June he ordered that the death sentence be revoked due to insufficient evidence. Three days later he exonerated Henry completely and ordered that he return to his duties. A newspaper report headlined 'Back to duty after quashed death verdict' appeared on 22 June, less than a month after the court martial and less than two months since the incident took place.

In the heat of wartime a potential wrong had been righted as speedily as it had been made. And it was all down to the strength of public feeling and the power of the press which, for once at least, had been deployed to good effect. I found Leroy Henry's story as reassuring as it was surprising. At a time when segregation laws in the United States oppressed millions – and would continue to do so until the 1960s – an African American gained justice here despite his colour. I would have expected the British public of the 1940s to be more inclined to racist attitudes than today's society – certainly indifferent to the guilt or otherwise of just one foreign soldier in the midst of war. But a sense of common justice won the day and saved a life.

There doesn't seem to have been much common justice in the case of Ben Gunn. While I was visiting other parts of the prison and uncovering its rich layers of history, he had been spending time alone here, coming to terms with being back in the institution where he had been locked up for so many years. I had arranged to rejoin him in the courtyard so we could go together to his old cell, B3/30. He seemed much more composed now, having done some exploring for himself. 'There's a fireplace in the corner of the wing office which had been covered up,' he said excitedly. 'I didn't know it was there. It means there's a shaft all the way to the roof, which we may have been interested in …' We entered B Wing, where he had lived, and climbed the metal stairs to the third landing. As he approached his former cell, number 30, he began to breathe deeply. 'Just seeing it, just being here,' he explained. I asked him how long he would spend locked up each day. 'Sixteen, seventeen, eighteen hours, depending,' was his reply.

In the cell Ben crouched on the floor by the old bed frame and I perched on the edge of the frame. The bald facts of his case are that he pleaded guilty to his friend's murder and was sentenced to a minimum of ten years in gaol. But the authorities kept pushing back his release date and his sentence came to seem never-ending. As time passed it wasn't so much the physical barriers that intimidated him as the apparently insurmountable wall of that sentence. 'If you're serving a fixed term, every day you can tick another day off, you know you're one day closer to your sentence ending and you can go home,' he said. 'With a lifer you could be there forever. You just don't know.'

At this point Ben revealed a crucial detail of his case that put everything in a different light: he was just fourteen years of age at the time of his friend's death. 'We were both in care. He was my room-mate in the kids' home. I happened to be holding a piece of wood. He didn't. He died.' The killing, he said, was entirely unintentional. 'I didn't mean to cause serious harm. But I did. As soon as I realized I went to the police. Phone box, nine nine nine. We went from there. He died a couple of days later.'

There was silence in the cell while I digested this information. My initial reaction was that Ben seemed remarkably free of self-pity despite the circumstances of his life at the time. He told me that his mother had died when he was nine, which was why he was living in a children's home when he committed the offence. Such institutions could be notoriously difficult environments in which young children received little affection and had no defence against exploitation and abuse by adults. He was also terribly young to have been convicted of the offence of murder.

He was, however, well above the age of criminal responsibility – the age under which children cannot be charged with and convicted of a crime. In England and Wales, this is fixed at ten years old (the age at which Robert Thompson and Jon Venables became the youngest murderers in English history when they killed the toddler James Bulger in 1993). In Europe the average is fourteen years old. But Ben did not seem interested in 'blaming the system'. 'No, no, no,' he said. 'Life and circumstance can lead you to a situation. How you deal with those circumstances – that's you. I killed my mate. Guilty. That's that.'

The most notorious juvenile killer in British criminal history was Mary Bell, who as a ten- and eleven-year-old strangled two toddlers in Newcastle-upon-Tyne in 1968. She was found guilty of manslaughter on the grounds of diminished responsibility and served twelve years. As a bewildered young teenager, Ben was advised to plead guilty to the charge of murder. 'That was my barrister's advice,' he told me. 'I first met my barrister fifteen minutes before I went into court. He came into the cell, said, "I'm your barrister, you've left me nothing to do, you've got to go up and plead guilty." So I went up and pleaded guilty.

'I wasn't looking at the legal subtleties – the difference between, say, manslaughter, which would have given me a six-year fixed sentence, or a life sentence which turned into thirty-two years. I didn't realize any of those things. But it's not something I've argued over, it really isn't. I know there is a legal argument to be made but I've never made it.'

If Ben was philosophical about his murder conviction, he expressed strong views about prison itself. A prison sentence is supposed to fulfil a variety of functions – among them to both punish and rehabilitate offenders, deter crime, and protect society by removing criminals from it. Ben had a different way of looking at incarceration. The system, he said, was 'for making everybody else feel better'. He had worked out that it had cost the taxpayer £1.4 million to put him away for over three decades – 'but I don't think you got your money's worth'. And I, as a former Chief Secretary to the Treasury, would have to concede that his point was well made. He also identified a paradox at the heart of the system: 'You can't have punishment and rehabilitation simultaneously. You can't punch someone in the mouth and give them a Band-Aid. You can't hurt and heal.'

Questions of crime and punishment have exercised many minds down the centuries, from Plato in ancient Greece to the prime minister whose Cabinet I served in. Reflecting on the criminal justice system in 1993, John Major suggested that 'Society needs to condemn a little more and understand a little less.' Was Ben a victim of such an approach? If he was, he disarmed me with his lack of bitterness. Having spent a lengthy sentence (years that took him from child to adult, bypassing all the productive and exciting milestones of a person living an averagely fulfilling life on the outside) in a world measuring five paces by ten, he has unequivocally accepted responsibility for his crime even though he was only fourteen years old when he committed it. At the same time he will always doubt what good it did him, what the point of it all was.

It's a question that some people prefer to avoid. Discovering some of Shepton Mallet's hidden history was making me re-examine my own thoughts about prison. Not only did the gaol fail to rehabilitate its most infamous inmates, the Krays, but it also swept them along on their life of crime. For Ben Gunn, gaol meant thirty-two years in a harsh environment that for much of the time was not conducive to preparing him for life on the outside. He was not, by his own account, a model prisoner. He questioned the purpose of being locked up and did not acquiesce easily to authority – which perhaps explains why it took so long for the authorities to sanction his release.

'The Parole Board for over a decade was recommending a move to open prison, pending release, and ministers were overruling it,' he said. One reason cited was that he had depression, which increased the chance of his reoffending. 'But hang on,' he said. 'The only psychiatric report they had said I suffered from depression and that *reduced* my risk of reoffending.' The real reason, he said, was that he was a paid-up member of the Awkward Squad: 'It's all games within games.'

In desperation he went on hunger strike at one point, but eventually found a way forward. To explain this latter part of his life in prison Ben took me to Shepton Mallet's modern annexe, built in the 1970s, where the architecture of wide corridors and big windows was far less oppressive. Signs pointing to 'Library' and 'Education' reflected the purpose of this new wing. We passed a suite of rooms where prisoners used to practise their painting and decorating skills, then climbed some stairs to a series of classrooms. 'This is my stomping ground – more specifically *there*,' he said pointing into a particular room. He was grinning from ear to ear. 'This where I met my partner,' he said. His *partner*? Not for the first time, Ben had surprised me. 'It was frowned upon,' he admitted. 'She was just a random woman teacher, teaching. I used to wander into her class, chat to my mates and just walk out. I was profoundly rude.'

Ben gained a degree in politics and history and a Masters in peace and reconciliation during his time at Shepton Mallet.

Then, in 2007, he met Alex, the 'remarkable woman' who would turn his life around. They got on badly at first but when she was put in charge of the prison magazine, a project that interested him, the mood quickly changed. 'This was our main room,' he said, looking truly relaxed for the first time. 'I'd sit in the corner, she'd have the desk there. We'd be passing little love notes to each other on Post-its. The whole room knew what was happening but no one said a word.' His eyes were twinkling. 'There was a convenient stationery cupboard.' He took me to it – a narrow room, with empty shelves now, but perfectly big enough for their purposes.

When they were eventually rumbled Alex was dismissed, but they remained in contact and she encouraged Ben to write a blog on prison life. The first one started with this rhetorical question: 'Where else can you sit around and pass the days chatting with people who have maimed, mutilated, molested and murdered?' Sensing for the first time that a meaningful future may await him on the outside, Ben changed his attitude and pressed to be released. On 23 August 2012 he finally walked free and Alex was waiting for him. Since then they have remained together and he has worked as a campaigner and commentator on the prison system. Emotionally, he admitted, things have not been plain sailing but he keeps trying to do his best. 'I just owe it to everybody to try and do a good job of life.' He paused, then added, 'Somehow.'

Ben and I were as relieved as each other when the doors of Shepton Mallet nick banged closed behind us to leave us back on the outside, free in body and soul. Everything I learned in there confirmed to me that prison is a terrible fate for any person, especially when the bureaucratic machinery of punishment grinds on regardless of common justice. The history of Shepton Mallet is also a microcosm of Britain's social history. It exemplifies how public attitudes and official policy on the thorny questions of crime and punishment have muddled very gradually towards more humane practice. And on a personal level maybe I laid some ghosts thanks to meeting Ben Gunn. For he lived the reality of my recurring 'prison' nightmare a thousand times over, yet each day found a way to go on. He struck me as a man of rare moral insight. Not, I think, *because* of the prison system, but in spite of it.

London Road Fire and Police Station, Manchester

Lying immediately to the west of Piccadilly railway station in the centre of Manchester is an Edwardian extravaganza of a building that occupies an entire city block. This startling structure of brick and terracotta, with turrets and domes and a tall belfry tower, could have been one of those grand railway hotels in the tradition of St Pancras in London. In fact it was once the heart and home of a breed apart. The clue is written across the lintel above the grand central archway: FIRE STATION.

This is, or was, the London Road Fire Station but, as I was about to discover, it wasn't a common or garden fire station, just a place to provide parking for the fire engines and a mess room for the crew. In its time it was one of the most significant firefighting centres in the country. It also served the community in other unexpected ways. These old bricks embody the spirit of people whom society may take for granted until it needs them:

individuals who hold the line between chaos and order; who run towards danger when the rest of us flee; who save our lives at risk to their own.

Access was through the pedestrian door recessed in one of the main wooden gates. The archway beyond led into an inner courtyard where scores of men and women were milling about in the convivial way of old friends and colleagues. A pipe band was playing 'Scotland the Brave' and as the kilted pipers and drummers finished the tune and started another, the crowd applauded – the band was kith and kin as the musicians in question comprised the Greater Manchester Fire and Rescue Service Pipe Band.

A plastic cup of pop was thrust into my hand, a plate of samosas and sausage rolls offered – and I was absorbed into a hubbub of reminiscence and comradeship. 'It's quite emotional for me,' said one man of perhaps my own age. 'I'm the third generation of my family who worked at this fire station.' Another even managed to wax lyrical about cleaning duties: 'Every Saturday I'd scrub all the yard, all the balconies – everywhere, up and down, it was scrubbed and then jetted with a hosepipe. It was immaculate. You could eat your dinner off the balconies.'

I had wandered into a party that was to feel more like a wake. This close-knit group of men and women were in such an expansive and nostalgic mood because it was the final gathering they would have here, where they had all once worked, and in some cases it was possibly the last time they would see each other again. The London Road Fire Station was decommissioned in 1986 and has lain empty and unused ever since, except for occasional get-togethers like this. But plans were now well underway to develop the site. Soon the old place would be gutted and reinvented as a complex of flats, offices and a hotel. The people who remembered it so fondly were paying their final respects.

The timing was lucky for me. It was a great privilege to be allowed access to this extraordinary building, for not only is it fascinating in architectural and functional terms but it also contains a wealth of stories concerning the history of 'first responders' in this country, not to mention tales of individual heroism. I also hoped to learn something of the special qualities of these unsung people, whose function in society (in the words of one former firefighter I met) is to 'save life, save property and render humanitarian services'.

The day after the farewell event I returned to explore the place in peace and quiet, and the first thing that struck me was the sheer size of the site. My idea of a fire station is a box of a building with big red doors, enough room inside for a couple of appliances, and a tower and operations room attached. The London Road station is a triangular-shaped citadel, an enclosed city within a city, rising to four storeys and lavishly decorated with carved nymphs, bearded faces and imperious eagles. In the inner courtyard there are iron balconies on three levels.

I pushed open a door on the far side of the courtyard and climbed stairs to the first floor. Here the first room I entered had a fireplace, which gave it a domesticated air. In the second there were cartoon characters painted on the walls and I stooped to retrieve a pair of toy drumsticks from the floor – a child's bedroom, surely. In the third room, where plaster was peeling from the walls, I had arranged to meet a couple of people who could explain precisely where I was.

'Welcome to our lovely abode!' said Barrie Pestle.

'If we'd known you were coming, we'd have decorated a bit more!' added Mike Berry.

The two of them had grown up here. They told me that London Road was a residential fire station, that we were standing in one of thirty-two flats provided for firefighters and their families, and that they both lived here as the sons of firefighters. 'I spent the first eleven years of my life here,' said Mike. He produced a photograph of himself taken in the courtyard when he was nine or ten years of age, wearing a junior fireman's uniform and holding a fire hose. 'It was a little community, like a village. Everybody looked after each other. Loads of kids. There were kids in almost every flat.'

It was, they agreed, an exciting place to live as children. When we returned to the courtyard Mike pointed up at the tall tower near the south-east corner, decorated at the very top with stone eagles perched on globes. This was the 'hose tower' and despite its dramatic embellishments it had a practical purpose: it was where they hung the fire hoses to dry after washing them. 'Sometimes if the firemen left the building open, if they went out on a fire call and forgot to lock it, I'd go up there, right up to the top,' said Mike. 'There's a drop there of over a hundred feet.' He grinned at the memory.

All this was a surprise to me. I had assumed that before the 1970s or early 1980s – when women were allowed to join the service and the correct descriptive noun changed from 'fireman' to 'firefighter' – a fire station had been a very adult male environment. London Road certainly had a well-appointed gymnasium up on the corner of the second floor, which Mike and Barrie took me to see. It's empty now but must have been a splendid space in its time, with a high ceiling and large windows overlooking London Road and Whitworth Street, where you could imagine fine physical specimens keeping themselves in shape in order to manage the arduous demands of fighting fires.

But with flats occupying the upper floors on all three sides, the London Road station was also a domesticated place, smelling of roast dinners on a Sunday, resounding to the theme tune of *Coronation Street* on weekday evenings and ringing with children's laughter pretty much all the time. 'The kids used to play on the wide balconies,' said Mike. 'Football, cricket. The ball going over into the yard and we'd be shouting at the firemen, "Throw my ball back!"'

'Which they would do,' added Barrie. 'They were very good to us.'

The fire service has always attracted a distinct type of community-minded person. Until the early nineteenth century firefighting was carried out by local voluntary brigades or teams contracted by insurance companies. Throughout the country old buildings still bear 'fire marks', the metal plaques placed high up on the frontage that indicated they were covered by insurance in the event of fire. If buildings were uninsured they were simply left to burn, but this was a highly unsatisfactory arrangement as fire did not discriminate between insured and uninsured buildings – having set the latter ablaze it would frequently engulf the former.

By the time London Road was built, between 1904 and 1906, the need for a universal service had been recognized and the responsibility for firefighting had passed to local government. The station wasn't just ambitious in design – it became, in modern parlance, a kind of 'one-stop shop' for death and disaster on the streets of Manchester by incorporating a police station and a coroner's court (which I would explore later in the day).

The residential element was common in big-city fire stations at the time, as firemen had to be on constant alert for immediate turnout (and indeed there were alarm bells in each flat). But living on top of each other in this way had another function. It fostered a sense of togetherness and trust that was vital in the life-threatening situations in which they would sometimes find themselves when fighting fires.

The fire service became one of those closed professions that tends to pass down the generations. Both Barrie and Mike, having grown up at London Road as the sons of firefighters, went on to join the profession themselves and to serve in this very station. But lest this all sounds rather too neat and cosy, they soon reminded me of the sometimes traumatic reality of their work. 'When you've had a child fatality, they're the worst ones,' said Mike. 'You don't get over them for a while. You just relate them to your own kids.'

The greatest incidence of fatalities – of both civilians and fire officers – occurred during the Second World War, when crew numbers were increased tenfold with volunteers to cope with the threat of air raids. The Luftwaffe's targets in Manchester included the A. V. Roe factory, which built Lancaster bombers, as well as aeronautical engine manufacturers, warehouses and highly combustible textile mills. Down in the courtyard a vision of those days appeared – a red Dennis fire engine with snout-like silver bonnet and wheeled ladder. 'It was delivered here in 1940,' explained the driver, Bob Bonner, as he descended from the open cab. 'It had a real baptism of fire, then spent the rest of its career at this fire station.'

Bob, a former firefighter and now a historian of the fire service, was based here himself, having joined the brigade as a sixteen-year-old. His father, Robert Bonner, served here for forty years, including the war years (1939–45) when according to Bob it was 'just complete pandemonium really'. The vintage Dennis, and the blue serge uniform Bob was wearing, are period pieces now. He talked affectionately of both. 'The engine has a pump and what we call a wheeled escape ladder – those are the original ladders that go back to Victorian times,' he said.

The uniform – which comprised a double-breasted jacket with silver buttons, wide-buckled belt and hard helmet with protective peaks front and back – remained essentially unchanged from the mid-nineteenth century to 'well into the 1960s'. He had brought along a similar uniform for me to try on and as I muttered the words, 'It's a great honour,' I meant it. Of the various careers I have pursued, from politician to broadcaster, none has involved my having to lay my life on the line for others, and I have great respect and admiration for those who face this prospect every working day.

I pulled on the jacket – the heavy woollen fabric, incidentally, can't have afforded much protection against fire – and buckled up the belt, attached to which was an axe used for breaking down doors and windows. 'One more thing, then you'll look like a fireman,' said Bob, planting a helmet on my head. 'OK, let's mount, as we say.' And while he climbed behind the large steering wheel, I sat in the passenger seat where the captain would normally sit. Then, channelling my inner nine-year-old, I rang the brass bell like crazy and we headed off into the streets of central Manchester for a spin.

This may sound like an exercise in harmless nostalgia but there was a serious point to it. Bob wished me to gain at least an inkling of what it must have been like for his father and fellow wartime firemen when they drove in a vehicle like this to a warehouse or factory blitzed by German incendiary bombs. Astonishingly, the firefighters of this era had barely any training. They learned on the job. And war was the most extreme and unforgiving of practice grounds.

'Once the air raids started in earnest there were larger fires than they'd ever experienced,' said Bob, as we rattled past the railway station (which was badly damaged in the war). 'The Christmas Blitz of 1940 was the big one. Two nights of severe bombing: December the twenty-second and twenty-third. In those two nights most of the damage and casualties occurred.' Some 470 tons of high explosive were dropped in that period. An estimated 684 people died and more than 2,000 were injured.

The old Dennis fire engine drew many admiring glances even if it was not the ideal vehicle for negotiating twenty-first-century traffic systems. When we returned it to the sanctuary of the London Road courtyard, Bob showed me a relic of Manchester's Christmas Blitz that brought home its absolute hellishness. 'It's what they call a branch pipe, which is the bit the firemen hold at the end of the hose,' he explained. 'Two firemen in Old Trafford were directing this onto a fire where incendiary bombs had set a church alight. The German bombers came back on a second air raid, dropped high-explosive bombs on the fire. The two firemen were killed, sadly. Roy Skelton and William Varah. This branch pipe was pretty much all that was found.' Bob offered me the pipe and I turned it in my hands. It was almost as long as my forearm and made of brass – a heavy, substantial object. But it had been penetrated by shrapnel and twisted by heat. We fell momentarily silent. Skelton and Varah were two of thirty Manchester firefighters killed in the Second World War.

In the post-war years the fire service was determined to act on lessons learned so harshly in wartime. The service was professionalized. Firefighters were no longer expected to pick it up as they went along. In 1948 one of Britain's premier firefighting schools was opened on the London Road site. One of its pupils was my next witness, Sam Smart, who joined me in the courtyard. 'I did three months' training here and I lived here so, yes, this has got a lot of memories for me,' he acknowledged.

In a career spanning thirty years Sam attended 9,000 blazes, so I knew I was in safe hands when he revealed that he planned to give me a taste of the training programme. First of all he handed me a uniform that post-dated the heavy serge jacket I had worn with Bob Bonner. It was called the Inferno suit and was in use until 2010. A faded maroon colour with fluorescent flashes, it was certainly bulky but was both water- and fireproof. Fortunately Sam didn't expect me to actually perform the first exercise he described.

'We used to have to do a height test,' he said. 'The instructor put the letter L and the letter R on the soles of your boots. He then asked you to walk to the top of the tower. See the three windows? The ledge above it?' I looked up – he was talking about a spot a good 70 feet from the ground. 'That's the edge of the tower. You couldn't come back down till the instructor had stood below and seen the L and R on the bottom of your boots.' I asked him if he was scared: 'Yes. A fireman who tells you he is not scared is a liar.'

Firefighters, he explained, have to be able to work at extreme heights, in confined spaces, while managing potentially dangerous equipment. Handling the hose correctly is a critical part of the job, as he was about to demonstrate. He handed me a coil of hose from the modern appliance he had brought along and showed me how to hold it in the middle and walk so it unspooled smoothly behind me. 'Now you want something to extinguish the fire – a branch.' This one was not made of brass, like the war relic, but of heavy-duty plastic which clicked easily into the fitting on the end of the hose.

'You're going to be aiming for that corner of the building,' said Sam. 'Your stance is left foot forward and right foot back. My stance is going to be behind you, same way.' I gripped the handle of the branch, which was like the stock of a pistol, with my right hand and steadied it with my left. 'Full power!' yelled Sam to a colleague on the appliance. The flat hose bulged to life, the branch recoiled in my hands. The force of the jet was enormous, the feel of that power beneath my hands unexpectedly exhilarating. This was only a medium-sized hose but it blasted out hundreds of litres of water a minute.

Controlling it was also challenging, even with Sam backing me up, supporting my shoulders. If a firefighter mishandles or loses control of the hose, the pressure could be enough to whip him or her up into the air or be thrown off a ladder. Factor in flames, fumes, smoke and panicking victims and you begin to understand the predicament of a firefighter in an extreme situation, and to appreciate the expertise required to be able to cope with it. The other thing that struck me was how much I relied on my colleague steadying the ship behind me. Firefighting is not a matter of individual heroics, but of working as a team in the service of collective safety and efficiency. Comradeship is all.

There is only so much training you can do, however. You can learn to operate equipment, prepare for flames and fumes. But what about the ultimate test, of having to deal with dead or dying victims? The next person I had arranged to meet was Paul Miller, who had barely finished his training at London Road when he attended the worst fire in Manchester since the Second World War. He told the story as we stood in the old engine room, complete with firemen's poles, where engines were once parked in a row between the pillars.

The year was 1979. At lunchtime on 8 May a clerk in the office of a taxi firm dialled 999 to report smoke coming from the Woolworth store at Piccadilly Gardens, a short distance north-west of the fire station. It was immediately apparent that the fire was huge and particularly problematic. 'The officer in charge made it "Pumps Ten" – ten engines straightaway,' recalled Paul.

There were some 500 customers in the store at the time. Many remained trapped inside as smoke billowed from all six storeys. Paul was a rookie, but not even the seasoned officers around him had experienced a conflagration of this magnitude. 'You're conditioned to do exactly what you're told to do, and that's basically all I did,' he said modestly. 'We got the ladders off to where there were some ladies trapped in the wages room. The window had iron bars on it so they couldn't get out. I will always remember the screams and the harrowing noises they made.'

Eventually a colleague cut through the bars with a reciprocating saw and freed the women. They survived but ten people died in the Woolworth fire – not in the flames, but from inhaling toxic fumes created by the burning synthetic fabrics and furnishings. Paul was one of the firemen tasked with recovering the bodies: 'We had to go up into the smoke, take one of the casualties, place them in a salvage sheet and bring them down to ground-floor level.' He had not seen a dead body before that day and admitted, with understatement, that it was 'a bit overwhelming'.

The fire at Grenfell Tower in west London in 2017 brought home to the entire nation the terrible psychological consequences for those caught up in such an inferno. Back in 1979 there was simply no provision for the emotional welfare of either victims or firefighters – even a youth of such inexperience as Paul Miller. But London Road had learned to look after its own. The female operators in the control room, who took emergency calls and dispatched the appliances to the fires, were very much part of the station's tight and mutually supportive community. One of their unofficial roles was to be good listeners to firemen who had returned from distressing call-outs.

Three of those operators, Linda Bonner, Gloria Gaffney and Lynne Bairsto met me in the old wood-panelled control room on the ground floor, where they once sat wearing headsets, listening and talking to citizens of a big city in their most vulnerable moments. They ran through the procedure for taking calls. 'You always had to get the address, the street number, the nearest main road and the locality,' said Gloria. 'They would sometimes say, "Oh, I don't know," and the only other thing we could ask was "Where is the nearest public house?" Everyone, after all, knows the name of their local.'

Most incidents were minor and easily dealt with, but occasionally there would be one of such severity that it threatened real psychological damage to the firefighters involved. 'I remember one incident, it was the Christmas period,' said Gloria. 'There was a fire and fatalities with children. I think there were three. That was awful because the fireman who carried them out said he had children of a similar age.'

This was where the operators came in. 'The firemen used to come in and sit with us, and we used to give them tea,' said Linda. 'And they talked out their problems. They never took their problems home. We were their counsellors.'

It wasn't just the firefighters at the London Road site who faced death and disaster. The history of this extraordinary Edwardian Baroque building in the centre of Manchester tends to be dominated by its association with the fire service, but as I explored its nooks and crannies further I found evidence of other functions, other equally fascinating worlds. On London Road I entered the building through a modest-looking wooden door, pushed through interior double doors glazed with stained glass and descended an ornate staircase to a basement waiting room lined with wooden benches and dimly lit by street-level grilles. Beyond it was a courtroom, a seemingly perfectly preserved capsule of Edwardiana with parquet flooring and wood-panelled walls. On the desk were old forms pertaining to deceased persons, requiring name, occupation and other details, which confirmed this as the former coroner's court, last used in 1998.

At street level I walked back along London Road, turned left into Whitworth Street and down at the bottom end I entered another section of the building, into a lobby of green-glazed brickwork. A succession of rooms led to a row of cells, with white-tiled walls, a bench and a lavatory. Sitting in one (entirely of his own volition, I should point out) and awaiting my arrival, was eighty-nine-year-old Dennis Wood, who had worked at London Road for twenty-five years. Dennis was a policeman based at the police station that was also sited here and we talked in one of the holding cells.

He said the police officers and firefighters who both operated from this building frequently found themselves working on the same cases – especially when fires had claimed lives or criminal intent was suspected. But the police station was busy in its own right, and the investigation that stands out for Dennis is one that will be immediately and chillingly familiar to all readers of this book.

'I was told to go round to a house where a little girl had gone missing,' he told me. 'Her mother was distraught.' The girl's name was Lesley Ann Downey, she was ten years old and she had disappeared after visiting a fairground on Boxing Day 1964. Subsequently she was revealed to have been one of the five victims of the so-called Moors Murderers, Myra Hindley and Ian Brady, two of the most cruel and depraved killers in British criminal history. Hindley was from the Gorton area of the city, to the south-east of the London Road fire and police stations. Once Brady and Hindley had been arrested, in October 1965, officers at this station were part of the team that painstakingly built the case against them, resulting in murder convictions and life sentences for both.

In 1981 the police had to contain riots in the local community – with their firefighter colleagues at London Road also targeted. One of the latter was Albert Gilbert and, as we talked back in the engine room, he admitted it had been a 'surreal' and entirely unfamiliar experience to be the object of such hostility. The occasion was the so-called Moss Side Riots which took place between 8 and 11 July 1981, when the deprived neighbourhood of Moss Side erupted in violent behaviour. There had been considerable sympathy among the firefighters for the plight of people in such inner-city areas, which were suffering high levels of unemployment and a general sense of hopelessness in the early 1980s. But they didn't expect to have missiles thrown at them.

'You'd got these shops with their windows put through and we started fighting the fire and a lad came along and said, "It's all kicking off, you'd better get out of here,"' recalled Albert. 'Next thing is we've got bricks and bottles coming towards us.' It was a hard way of learning a crucial truth about the first responders of the fire service. They do their job without fear or favour and act at all times with impartiality. 'You don't have any control over what happens, you just do what you've signed up to do,' Albert told me. 'That is, save life, save property, render humanitarian services. And humanitarian services can cover a multitude, including riots.' He allowed himself a wry smile.

In 1986, five years after the Moss Side Riots, Manchester's London Road Fire Station closed for good. It was the usual story – the building was too costly to maintain and no longer commensurate with the demands of modern firefighting, which had devolved to smaller neighbourhood stations. After lying empty for thirty years and deteriorating accordingly, it is now going to be developed as a complex of apartments, offices, 'cultural spaces' and a 'boutique hotel'.

This fate is hardly unusual, but in many cases the redevelopment of historic sites pays only lip service to their cultural heritage. The developers of London Road seem intent on incorporating as much as possible of the original fabric and history, however, and a representative of the development company, Rochelle Silverstein, was enthusiastically persuasive when she came along to the site to explain the scheme more fully.

'We have really taken our time over it,' she said, as we stood on one of the balconies where firefighters' children once played. 'We are meticulously going round the building documenting every single finish, every single window, to see what we can keep and what we can bring back to life. We've taken lots of histories from people who lived here and we want to document them in one place if we can.'

Artists have been brought in to introduce a uniquely creative element to this commemorative process. One such is Harriet Shooter-Redfearn, who I found beavering away in one of the old flats. She records tiny and apparently ephemeral traces of people's lives and preserves them. In this case it was firemen's signatures that she had found scribbled on walls beneath wallpaper. She recreates them in wire and embeds the wire in glass to make a sculpture.

'My dad's a firefighter, so there's a personal connection,' she told me. 'Through this building we can access stories about the community. I feel the community is really important and it's something we are perhaps losing in contemporary society.'

Harriet hit the nail on the head with this comment. The men and women who called London Road home were a true community, a community within a community, who lived, worked and in some cases died together. Behind these citadel-like walls they fostered the comradeship that enabled them to go out into the wider world and make it a safer, kinder place for the rest of us. Founded on mutual trust and courage, they were the best sort of family.

PART II

Life and Death

It was known as a 'Blighty wound' – an injury sustained in the trenches of the First World War that was considered serious enough to require treatment back in 'Blighty', meaning Britain. Trapped in the horrors of the Western Front, some soldiers yearned for such a wound so long as it was not life-threatening or life-changing. But many returned with injuries so appalling and disfiguring they might have wished they'd been left to die in the mud and havoc.

I thought of these shattered young men as I stood outside Cambridge Military Hospital in Aldershot, one of the three sites I explore in this section (the others being the Royal London Hospital in the East End of London and the sewers beneath the seaside town of Brighton). Each represents an important step change in our knowledge of medicine and health in Britain.

You may think I chose Cambridge Military Hospital because of its pioneering surgical work in fixing broken soldiers. That was indeed my initial assumption and motivation. The Cambridge was one of the specialist hospitals to which the worst cases of physical disfigurement were repatriated during the First World War. Built on a hill, it dominates the surrounding landscape as Britain dominated much of the globe when the hospital admitted its first patients twenty-one years before the turn of the twentieth century. It is a statement of power and greatness, telling the world that nothing but the finest treatment and surroundings will do for men who have served queen and country, and put their lives on the line for Empire.

I felt a particular affinity for the Cambridge, probably because it reflects a tradition that goes back to King Charles II and the Royal Hospital at Chelsea, where I have attended many parades and events as the constituency MP. Before the king commissioned the Chelsea hospital, which opened in 1692, the state did not take responsibility for injured soldiers or those who had fallen on hard times. The magnificent hospital designed and built by Sir Christopher Wren on the banks of the Thames, in what was then open countryside, expressed the gratitude of a nation for its fighting men. (This was in turn inspired by the Hôtel des Invalides, the complex of buildings authorized by Louis XIV and completed in Paris in 1676. Both the Chelsea hospital and Les Invalides still serve as retirement homes for old soldiers.)

Not only does Cambridge Military Hospital catch the eye, but it also harmonizes design and function. Its long spinal corridor provided easy access for busy nurses shuttling between different departments. The wards were high-ceilinged, with large windows admitting plenty of healthy and cheering natural light. For those men returning from the hell of the trenches it must have seemed a haven of organization and optimism. And the work that took place there, under the authority of the plastic surgeon Harold Gillies, was truly astounding. But the story that arose out of Gillies' work at the Cambridge Hospital was not, in the end, the one I had expected to hear.

It's a riveting narrative that I shall leave you to discover in the chapter proper but it does serve to illustrate a truism about medicine: that the most innovative medical practice often takes place in the most challenging of environments. In the years of the First World War and after, that was certainly true of Cambridge Military Hospital. And you could make the same case for the Royal London Hospital, in the nineteenth century especially.

While it was not located in a war zone, the Royal London, on the Whitechapel Road, did serve one of the most deprived areas of London, a neighbourhood of squalor and disease where, in the words of the American writer, Jack London, 'the obscenities and brute vulgarities of life are rampant'. It is no surprise that the doctors who worked there, the students of the medical college and the staff of the nursing school were at the forefront of best practice for over 250 years. Above all, it was a place of humanity, as hospitals should be. If there is one image that for me sums up the spirit of the Royal London, it is that of the 'Elephant Man', Joseph Merrick – a man even more hideously disfigured than the worst cases from the Western Front – and Frederick Treves – the eminent physician who looked after him – conversing as equals and friends in Merrick's basement rooms in the hospital.

Merrick's board and lodging at the London Hospital was paid for by a concerned public, following an appeal published in *The Times*. This arrangement echoed the charitable ethos of hospitals in medieval times, when they provided care and accommodation for the poor, the blind and the itinerant, as well as the sick. The London Hospital had opened in the mid-eighteenth century as a 'voluntary hospital', independently run and funded by contributions from wealthy individuals and philanthropic organizations. Similar hospitals opened in other parts of London, including Guy's in Southwark and the Middlesex in the West End, and across the country, from the Royal Infirmary in Edinburgh to Addenbrooke's in Cambridge. It's important to make this point because it shows that the principle of providing free healthcare to those who could not afford to pay predates the establishment of the National Health Service in 1948.

In the chapter on the Royal London Hospital I talk about the medical advances that took place there in the nineteenth century – not least in surgery, facilitated by a local supply of fresh corpses for students to practise on. Another crucial development was in the branch of medical science known as epidemiology. This, briefly, is the study of where and how diseases originate in a given population. The doctor credited with its creation is John

Snow, whose work in tracing the origins of a cholera outbreak in central London I refer to in the chapter on Brighton's sewers.

Before Snow demonstrated that cholera was being spread by water contaminated by sewage, it was generally thought that disease was transmitted by 'miasmas' or toxic vapours. No one thought to question the basic system of sewage disposal that emptied human waste in open channels directly into London's streams and rivers, which then emptied themselves into the Thames. John Snow died on 16 June 1858, just a few days before the stench of the Thames at Westminster grew so unbearable in the hot weather that it became known as the 'Great Stink'.

The Great Stink forced the government not just to hold its nose but to do something about the river of effluent that the Thames had become. Parliament resolved to create a modern sewerage system beneath the rapidly expanding metropolis and the man responsible for the design and implementation of this huge engineering project was the chief engineer at the Metropolitan Board of Works (the forerunner of the London County Council), Joseph Bazalgette.

Bazalgette tends to monopolize the story of sewers in Britain. But in towns and cities throughout the country Victorian engineers of comparable vision began building sewerage systems as part of a wider industrialization that has shaped modern Britain. Brighton was a particularly urgent case. After the arrival of the railway in 1841, the town billed as 'merry Dr Brighton' was looking increasingly green around the gills. Day trippers and fun seekers were arriving by the trainload and the basic sewerage systems couldn't cope. The result was polluted water sources and some of the worst outbreaks of cholera in the country – though you'd hardly have known it from news reports, as the tourist authorities kept a lid on the dire state of Brighton's public health.

The engineer responsible for the sewers beneath Brighton was John Hawkshaw and he had a hand in many significant infrastructure projects of the Victorian era, from the Severn Railway Tunnel to sections of the London Underground. Like everything the Victorians touched they were built to last and still work. I love the fact that Brighton's sewers are better built than the flashy Regency squares they underpin.

The Royal London Hospital

There's surely no more vibrant a city neighbourhood than the Whitechapel Road in the East End of London. I emerged from the Tube station into a teeming thoroughfare of people with faces and clothing from all over the world. The shops tucked below the old Victorian frontages were selling saris and exotic foodstuffs. A short walk west lies Whitechapel Gallery, where David Hockney had his first show, and Brick Lane, home to one of the world's most famous street markets. I may be a Londoner, born and bred, but this part of the capital is a far cry from Westminster and has always felt different and exciting to me.

On this occasion I wasn't here to look at paintings or eat delicious street food. The focus of my investigation was the block of old brick buildings across from the Tube station on the south side of the Whitechapel Road. The Georgian façade, with its gold lettering and clock high up in the pediment, once lent an air of elegance to the bustling street. Now it just looked abandoned. The windows were blanked out with hardboard, pigeons had used its ledges for target practice and weeds were sprouting.

The disrepair was a temporary state as the building was in the process of being repurposed as a new civic centre for the local council, Tower Hamlets. My interest lay in its original purpose, for this was the former London Hospital, which ministered to the sick and dying of this singular part of London for just over 250 years until it closed its doors in 2012. The hospital still exists – behind the old complex the Royal London Hospital (the regal handle was added in 1990 when Queen Elizabeth II visited) continues its work in a gleaming new edifice of blue glass.

Meanwhile the old wards and corridors, operating theatres and emergency rooms, were about to be gutted and rebuilt. Before this happened I needed to get in there and bear witness to the events of the past. For this was the scene of some of the most important breakthroughs in medical history, from anatomical research to X-rays. The hospital also provided an unlikely link between two of Victorian Britain's most compelling figures, the so-called 'Elephant Man' and the depraved serial killer known as Jack the Ripper. There was a lot of history to unravel here and I was anxious to get on with it.

But first, as I stood on the Whitechapel Road amid honking horns and spiced aromas, I needed to remind myself of the background picture. In the late 1880s, around the time that many of the surrounding shops and houses were being built, Queen Victoria had been on the British throne for more than fifty years, presiding over an era of unrivalled economic growth and prosperity. Britain's pre-eminence in the world was reflected in contemporaneous maps in which the countries of the British Empire, marked in pink, covered much of the globe.

Britannia truly did rule the waves, but not all her subjects lived lives that befitted such a powerful and successful nation. In 1889 another colour-coded map was published that told a different story about Britain. This was a 'poverty map' of London, produced by the social scientist and reformer Charles Booth, on which streets and neighbourhoods were coloured according to the wealth of the people who lived there. Before my visit to the Whitechapel Road I had studied it carefully online – and been shocked by what it revealed.

On Booth's map the West End of the late nineteenth century is coloured predominantly yellow and red, indicating 'wealthy' and 'well-to-do', but as one's eye tracks east and south, following the course of the Thames, the map darkens with patches of black and dark blue, representing the haunts of the 'lowest class' and 'very poor'. These dark areas are most concentrated in Southwark and the East End, inhabited by citizens characterized by Booth as 'vicious' and 'semi-criminal', and suffering 'chronic want'.

They lived in common lodging houses (the equivalent of night shelters) and slums known as 'rookeries', where disease was rife and mortality rates were sky-high. According to *The People of the Abyss,* a searing account of East End life by the American author Jack London, published in 1903, 'the obscenities and brute vulgarities of life are rampant. There is no privacy. The bad corrupts the good, and all fester together.'

I zoomed in on the online image of the map and took a closer look. On the south side of the Whitechapel Road, in the very heart of the 'abyss' described by Jack London, is a square of neutral grey which marked a beacon of hope. For here stood the charitable institution called the London Hospital, which, on its foundation in 1740, was dedicated to 'the relief of all sick and diseased persons and, in particular, manufacturers, seamen in the merchant service and their wives and children'.

Originally called the London Infirmary, it was the brainchild of several philanthropic businessmen who funded it by public subscription. Two hundred years before the launch of the National Health Service, the London Hospital was established precisely on the NHS principle of providing free healthcare irrespective of patients' ability to pay. Having occupied two sites, in Moorfield and Whitechapel, it relocated to the Whitechapel Road in the late 1750s. The people it served were among the most cosmopolitan as well as the poorest in Britain, representing successive waves of immigration – Huguenots originally from France, Jews of Spanish and Portuguese descent, more recent Jewish arrivals from the pogroms of Russia and Poland, labourers from all over Britain and Ireland, and several generations of East Londoners.

As I unlocked the hospital's old front door, and manhandled my way through 'automatic' sliding doors that had lost their electric power, I reflected that the hospital's role in this cosmopolitan society remained essentially the same down the years. And, as I hoped to demonstrate, the singular needs of a diverse and impoverished neighbourhood were precisely what drove its pursuit of medical excellence and innovation.

On initial inspection the old place was a derelict version of any NHS hospital you have visited featuring familiar signage ('Pharmacy', 'Haematology') and wards now emptied of their beds but with the wall-mounted anglepoise lamps still in place. The operating theatres still retained those powerful lights, resembling a giant insect's compound eyes. And in one I found an abandoned white clog, the footwear of choice for modern-day surgeons. But it felt as if this hospital that had seen so much was determined to feed me clues, for in one room I came across some photographic slides scattered across the floor. And when I stooped to pick one up I discovered that it showed a disfigured human face.

The photograph was probably taken within the last twenty years, presumably for training or educational purposes, but it provided me with an immediate and vivid link to an event in November 1884 and a story that reflects the true humanitarian spirit of the London Hospital. On that long-ago day in early winter, a young man made the same short journey that I had, from the north to the south side of the Whitechapel Road and into the hospital. It's a distance of just a few yards but this man didn't walk, he took a horse-drawn cab. And he was not wearing the usual street clothes of the day.

Instead he had on a long black cloak, voluminous slippers for his oversized feet and a peaked cap with a face veil. He was also carrying a calling card bearing the name of Frederick Treves, Lecturer on Anatomy at the London Hospital Medical College. The man was called Joseph Merrick and the clothes he wore were intended to disguise his profound physical deformities and spare him the horrified abuse of passers-by. He was better known then as the Elephant Man and though to many people he resembled a monster, he was far from monstrous. Rather, said Joanne Mungovin, 'he was a gentle gentleman. There's never been anyone like him.'

I had invited Joanne to the London Hospital to talk me through the Joseph Merrick story because she has a unique perspective. Not only is she from Leicester, Merrick's home city, but she is a descendant of Tom Norman, the Victorian impresario who exhibited the Elephant Man to the public. Human 'freak shows' were common in those days – people suffering from gigantism or dwarfism (such as the American performer 'General Tom Thumb'), 'bearded ladies', 'fat ladies', the limbless and multi-limbed could make a kind of living by agreeing to be gawped at. In 1884 Norman displayed the man he promoted as the Elephant Man in one of the shops that still exist near Whitechapel Tube Station (at the time of writing it's a branch of JD Sports).

The proximity to the London Hospital was fortuitous all round. Having dropped in to view the exhibit out of professional curiosity, a hospital doctor gave a graphic account of the Elephant Man to Frederick Treves, then an up-and-coming surgeon and anatomy lecturer, and suggested he take a look for himself. Treves was duly fascinated by what he saw and arranged for Merrick to come to the hospital for a proper medical examination. It was he who laid on the cab for the short journey and gave Merrick his calling card.

Joanne had brought along an original copy of the paper that Treves wrote based on his examinations of Merrick at this time, entitled 'A case of congenital deformity', which was published in *Transactions of the Pathological Society of London* in 1885. She opened it at a lithograph, taken from full-length photographs, showing Merrick from the front and the back. His right arm and leg are grotesquely enlarged. His left arm and shoulder, however, appear normal and hint at the trim figure Merrick might have been. The left arm, Treves noted, was 'a delicately shaped limb covered with fine skin and provided with a beautiful hand which any woman might have envied'.

Joanne also showed me a fascinating item she had borrowed from the Royal London Hospital Museum, the cap Merrick was wearing on the day he paid Treves a visit. It is peaked and could have belonged to, say, a railway-station porter of the time, except for its extraordinary size and the face veil sewn into it. 'His head was about thirty-eight inches in diameter,' she said, then pointed to the grey flannel mask beneath the peak. 'If you look there you can see the little pillar-box slits where his eyes would see through.'

For Treves, at this time, Merrick was little more than a fascinating medical specimen. He recorded the man's deformities with professional dispassion: the 'enormous and misshapen head'; the skin like 'a brown cauliflower'; the 'enormous' and 'shapeless' right arm; and so on. And after their encounter he continued on the upward trajectory of his medical career with no reason to believe their paths would cross again. But fate was to bring them together once more.

On the morning of 24 June 1886 Merrick was found collapsed at Liverpool Street Railway Station, having returned penniless from an ill-fated tour of the Continent during which his 'manager' had robbed and abandoned him. The policemen who attended him found Treves's calling card in his pocket and sent a message to the doctor requesting his help. So it was that Treves rescued Merrick and brought him the short distance back to the London Hospital.

Merrick was put up in an attic room as a temporary measure, but Treves soon realized he could not simply turf him out on to London's mean streets once he had recovered his health. So he spoke to the Chairman of the London Hospital, Francis Carr Gomm, who wrote a letter to *The Times* asking for help. It was, you might say, an example of Victorian crowdfunding, for the readers' generous response enabled the hospital to provide Merrick with a bed-sitting room in the basement of the East Wing and fund his board and lodging till his death in 1890.

The actions of Treves and the hospital authorities in offering sanctuary to Joseph Merrick were extremely enlightened for their day. As Joanne told me, 'The arrangement was incredibly unusual. This was a hospital for curing people, not a hospital for incurables.' Treves visited him every day, coming to realize that he was 'a gentle, affectionate and lovable creature'. And this touching friendship was also, in its way, a remarkable thing, a testament to the unique spirit of the London Hospital. For where else in Victorian Britain would a man at the pinnacle of society – subsequently made a knight and a baronet – sit down on equal terms with society's ultimate outcast? In 1887 Merrick entertained an even more socially exalted guest when Alexandra, Princess of Wales, dropped in to shake his hand after attending a ceremonial opening of new hospital premises. Merrick had achieved celebrity status and establishment approval – and the London Hospital enjoyed a certain reflected glory from its association with him.

The suite of rooms where Merrick passed his days – and from which, at Treves's insistence, all mirrors had been removed – was demolished a long time ago. But I was haunted by the thought of his circumscribed but relatively contented life here, strolling in the hospital garden on moonless nights and dreaming of one day living in a 'blind asylum' where his deformities could not be seen. He never realized his dreams of another life. He died at the London Hospital at the age of twenty-seven, probably of a broken neck due to the weight of his head.

The London Hospital, I was beginning to appreciate, was the kind of place where extraordinary stories accumulate, overlapping with other extraordinary stories. Much as he would be horrified by the idea, the gentle Elephant Man is linked to one of history's most reviled and depraved figures through his connection to this place. While Merrick, a man who appeared monstrous, was hiding his face and his gentle nature from the world, a short distance away a man whose countenance we will never know was demonstrating the actions of a true monster. I'm referring, of course, to the serial killer known as Jack the Ripper, whose killing fields were all within a mile of the hospital. Did Joseph Merrick, on his lonely night-time strolls in the hospital garden, pause to listen to distant cries from the surrounding streets and wonder what he was hearing?

The Jack the Ripper case has gone down as the most notorious in the history of criminology, not just in Britain but around the world. He was never unmasked and speculation as to his identity has fuelled a lucrative and usually sensationalistic industry in books and films that shows no sign of abating. Plausible suspects are thin on the ground but they include George Chapman, a Pole who changed his name from Seweryn Kłosowski (he is thought to have been living in the East End in 1888 and was hanged in 1903 for the murder, by poisoning, of three women unrelated to the Ripper case). The American crime writer Patricia Cornwell claims to have spent $7 million in pursuit of her theory that the artist Walter Sickert was the true perpetrator. I rather think the money could have been better spent. Among other unlikely names put forward over the years by writers with books to sell are the author Lewis Carroll and the philanthropist Thomas John Barnardo, of Dr Barnardo's fame, who studied medicine at the London Hospital.

I needed to bring some academic rigour to a case that, for all the millions of words expended on it, still felt out of focus. Was there a direct link between Jack the Ripper and the London Hospital? And what were the medical and criminological repercussions of the case? To answer these questions and lend their expert analysis I had enlisted the help of the historian and criminologist Dr Drew Gray, who specializes in nineteenth-century crime and punishment, and Dr Richard Shepherd, a consultant forensic pathologist who has conducted many autopsies at the London Hospital and is a student of the Ripper case.

'The London Hospital is part of the landscape of the Ripper killings,' said Drew, as we stood in its now unlit, deserted corridors. 'They all take place within this very small geographical area. It was a dangerous place to live. Brutal attacks on individuals, and particularly on prostitutes working at night, were quite common. There is quite a difference, of course, between the series of murders we associate with the killer known as Jack the Ripper and the more common everyday sort of murders because of the level of violence involved.'

The five killings generally attributed to the Ripper were committed over a ten-week period, starting on 31 August 1888 and concluding on 9 November. The victims – Mary Ann Nichols, Annie Chapman, Elizabeth Stride, Catherine Eddowes and Mary Jane Kelly – were all alcoholics who lived in local 'common lodging houses' (or, in the case of Kelly, a single room) and scraped a living from casual prostitution. All were mutilated and as the murder spree progressed, and the savagery of the mutilation increased, the fear and hysteria in the Whitechapel area intensified.

The killings would undoubtedly have been the talk of the London Hospital and there is a theory that the killer was a doctor or medical student at the hospital itself. 'The speed with which this person mutilates and takes out organs from the bodies – on the street, in dim lighting – suggests to me it's someone who knows what they're doing to some degree,' said Drew. 'Now whether that's a person who's medically trained – it's a difficult thing to judge. But I think there's something in it. A doctor might fit the bill.'

Drew had brought along a copy of a letter purporting to be from the Ripper himself. It was sent to the chairman of the Whitechapel Vigilance Committee, a local builder called George Lusk, a fortnight after the murder of Eddowes in mid-October. 'What's interesting about this letter is that it arrived with a small parcel attached,' he said. 'When Mr Lusk opened the parcel he found inside what seemed to be a piece of human kidney.' The barely literate note claimed this was 'half the Kidne I took from one women'. The letter writer, who signed off with 'Catch me when you can Mishter Lusk', claimed that he had fried and eaten the other half of the kidney and revealed that 'it was very nise'. To add to the Gothic tone, the address given at the top (and the name by which the letter has become known) was 'From hell'.

Lusk's initial reaction was to dismiss the package as a prank, perhaps perpetrated by a student at the London Hospital Medical College where the organs of dissected corpses could have been purloined relatively easily. Nevertheless Lusk took the specimen in the package to a local doctor whose assistant, Francis Reed, then took it to Dr Thomas Openshaw, the curator of the Pathology Museum at the London Hospital, for further examination.

There is some dispute about Dr Openshaw's findings. According to Reed and subsequent newspaper reports, the doctor had confirmed the specimen was part of the left kidney of a woman of about forty-five years old (Catherine Eddowes was forty-six) who was a heavy drinker. But Dr Openshaw himself, in a newspaper interview, was far more circumspect, stating merely that the specimen was half a human kidney, probably from the left side. It is significant that even in the midst of the killing spree the sensational aspects of the case were being played out and argued over in the press. The role of popular newspapers in fanning the flames of speculation helped to create the Ripper myth and set the tone for subsequent reporting of gruesome murders.

But Dr Openshaw's failure to arrive at harder conclusions about the nature and origin of the kidney in the package illustrates just how basic techniques in forensic medicine – the application of medical knowledge to establish the facts of a criminal case – were at the time of the Ripper killings.

No one is better qualified to disentangle medical fact from tabloid myth than the forensic pathologist Dr Richard Shepherd who in a long and distinguished career has acted as a consultant to the Bloody Sunday Inquiry and the investigation into the death of Diana, Princess of Wales. When I met him by the main reception desk he was shocked to find his old stomping ground devoid of life. 'Walking up here just now was very peculiar because I knew it when it was a very busy, active hospital,' he said. 'I was often here doing dissections.'

Richard sees the Ripper murders as a seminal case in the history of forensic medicine, which was at an embryonic stage in the late nineteenth century. 'They knew they needed to document injuries. They knew they needed to describe things. But they still weren't doing it to the standard we would want today,' he said. The case exposed the limitations of medical science and hastened the development of more sophisticated techniques that today form the backbone of criminal investigations. These include photographs and detailed records of crime scenes. Only one of the Ripper's victims (Mary Jane Kelly) was photographed where her body was found. The others were not photographed until their bodies had been taken to the mortuary. In the Catherine Eddowes case the police made drawings and plans of Mitre Square, where her body was discovered. Eddowes and Kelly were the final two of the five definitive Ripper victims, so it seems the police investigation became more thorough and professional as the case progressed.

In Richard's opinion the key medical fact common to all five of the murders was that they featured 'a cut throat – from left to right'. He has also detected a 'progression' in the severity of the mutilation which is common in serial killers. Mary Ann Nichols, the first victim, died of a cut throat and then suffered slash wounds to the abdomen. Eddowes had a kidney removed. 'In the fifth case [Kelly],' he pointed out, 'the body had been taken inside. It was in a tenement building, in a room. And what this means of course is that he's sure that he's not going to be disturbed. And that fifth body was extensively mutilated.'

As he talked Richard led me up to the third floor, where we entered one of the hospital's oldest operating theatres, purpose-built around the turn of the twentieth century with large windows designed to admit as much natural light as possible. He agreed that Jack the Ripper could well have had some anatomical expertise. 'But a lot of people could have had it. Abattoir workers, veterinary surgeons, doctors.'

By the late nineteenth century, the cutting up of human bodies had been the London Hospital's stock-in-trade for a century or more. 'The equipment hasn't changed much in hundreds of years,' said Richard, producing an old wooden box of bone-handled surgeon's instruments from the early 1800s. 'All it is is a set of scalpels and a pair of forceps. The reason they would have seven or eight scalpels in a box is that they would go blunt so quickly.'

Two hundred years ago such knives would have been wielded by a master surgeon in a theatre pretty much like this, as students stood in a gallery craning their necks for the best view. The study of medicine is reliant above all on knowledge of human anatomy. The only way to gain such knowledge is by dissecting recently deceased bodies, but fresh cadavers were often not readily available as few people would agree to having their mortal remains cut up after death – not least because the Christian churches taught that it might preclude their bodily resurrection.

'Pigs and other animals were very commonly used as a dissection tool in the sixteenth, seventeenth, eighteenth centuries,' said Richard. 'There still were huge problems in getting human bodies for dissection and that continued until 1752 with the Murder Act, which meant that bodies could be used – but only the bodies of people who had been executed [by hanging].'

Under the Murder Act the bodies of executed murderers could be taken away and used for public dissections. But this provision made hardly a dent in the shortfall in cadavers. Many anatomy schools resorted, instead, to the services of so-called 'Resurrectionists' – bodysnatchers who emptied graveyards up and down the country through the eighteenth and early nineteenth centuries. But even in death the class divide prevailed. The well-to-do took care to bury their dead in locked mausoleums or sealed lead coffins. The corpses of the poor, often buried in pauper's graves or obtainable through bribery, were far more accessible.

The Medical College at the London Hospital had become the country's first purpose-built medical school when it opened in a building next to the main hospital complex in 1785. Its high volume of patients and the broad variety of diseases and ailments they presented with made it a particularly good place to pioneer new ideas and train young doctors. It prided itself on the quality of its anatomical dissections and was no different from other establishments in doing backstreet deals with grave robbers. But it also had a source of bodies even closer to home than the cemeteries of the East End.

At this point in the story I left Richard to his memories of the London Hospital and stepped outside to keep an appointment and breathe some fresh air. The air proved to have something of a fetid flavour, however, as you might presently appreciate. I left the main hospital building by the back steps, which led down to a large, empty yard of puddles and weeds. Behind it, the new buildings of the Royal London Hospital rose in a dazzle of blue-green glass. Waiting for me in the middle of the yard was Louise Fowler, an archaeologist with the Museum of London who had made an astonishing discovery here a little over a decade ago.

'If you were standing on this spot in the early nineteenth century you'd have been in the burial ground that was attached to the hospital,' she told me. The site of this burial ground was well known – but what it contained proved a revelation when Fowler and her colleagues carried out an archaeological dig here in 2006. They recovered the remains of at least 259 people and traces of 111 coffins, dating from the first half of the nineteenth century. 'There was something quite unusual about some of the remains that we found in the coffins,' she said. 'We didn't just find burials of complete individuals. We also found dissected remains.' What had dumbfounded researchers was that half the men and a quarter of the women and children found in single graves had been cut up, while some coffins contained a mix of bones from several different men, women, children and foetuses.

Some of the bones were wired, indicating they had been used as models. Others had been sawed or nicked by scalpels. The conclusion, explained Fowler, was that 'at the London Hospital they were using the bodies of dead patients for anatomical demonstrations. The bodies were being buried in the burial ground and then they were being dug up at night and taken into the medical school.' This happened not just once or twice but as common practice: those who had died on hospital wards or in operating theatres were interred by day, exhumed by night, recycled through the Medical College for dissecting purposes and reburied once they had served their purpose – all with the collusion of the hospital authorities. There is also the suggestion that individuals within the hospital were profiting through the trade of these bodies to private medical schools.

Did patients understand what was going on? Did they watch the macabre spectacle of exhumations and reburials from their ward windows, in mortal terror of suffering the same fate? Contemplating this possibility, Louise and I both raised our eyes to the rows of hospital windows overlooking the yard. The windows were covered in hardboard – as if the hospital were maintaining a deliberately blank expression, refusing to admit this shameful episode of its past.

Medical progress, it seems, often comes at a cost – in this case the illegal, unethical practice of robbing its own dead from their graves and the horror felt by patients who feared for the future of their own mortal remains. In the case of the next breakthrough at the London Hospital, it was the doctors themselves who suffered. For centuries the only means of revealing the inner workings of the human body was to open it up with a scalpel – hence the unscrupulous trade in corpses. But at the end of 1895, at Würzburg in Germany, Professor Wilhelm Röntgen made an extraordinary discovery. Using electromagnetic radiation he created a 'ray' (he dubbed it 'X-ray') which produced an image of the inside of objects. His first proper X-ray was of his wife's hand and he realized immediately the revolutionary medical potential of this technique: for the first time the internal structure of the human body could be examined for diagnostic purposes without the need for surgery.

By 1896 doctors at the London Hospital were already experimenting with the new technique, using a shed in the garden where Joseph Merrick had walked just a decade earlier. I returned through the back door for an appointment with Dr Adrian Thomas, a radiographer and student of the history of radiography. He had brought along one of the very first X-ray machines, an unwieldy wooden tripod supporting a glass tube, and set it up in a side room. 'The problem with radiation is, it comes out in all directions,' he said, patting his antique machine. 'These early tubes had no protection around them which meant that everyone around was irradiated.'

The same applied to the next bit of kit he produced, an object that looked like a megaphone but was known as a 'cryptoscope'. It was a handheld X-ray device that enabled the doctor to view the patient in real time, without the need to record an image on glass, paper or plate. 'This imaging enabled us to make a diagnosis. The trouble was, both patient and physician were being irradiated,' said Adrian. The results were certainly groundbreaking. He produced a radiographic sheet and held it up to the light. This was an X-ray of a knee, taken at the London Hospital in the early twentieth century. 'Here's the fibula, with a tumour inside it,' he said, indicating a shadow where the bone joined the knee. But the pioneering radiographers who created such images were playing Russian roulette with their personal health. One of them was called Ernest Wilson and his dedication to medical investigation knew no bounds.

'People used their own hands as test objects,' said Adrian. 'What happened to Ernest Wilson is that he had progressive damage to his hands called radiodermatitis. It's like really bad sunburn that produces spasm and pain. Then his fingers began to show more severe changes and in a poignant way he took a series of X-rays that showed their progressive destruction.' Adrian revealed the actual X-rays to me, which clearly indicated how Wilson's hands and fingers had begun to disintegrate. Even as he fell critically ill, his capacity for objective self-analysis did not waver. 'In the end,' said Adrian, 'he had his hands amputated and then died from radiation malignancy.'

Ernest Wilson was one of four radiographers at the London

Hospital who sacrificed their lives to their pioneering work. Nowadays we may take the X-ray procedure completely for granted, but the next time I have one I'll certainly remember Wilson and his colleagues in this hospital – just some of the early radiographers who came to be known as the 'X-ray martyrs'.

Wilson's sacrifice was entirely in keeping with the spirit of this hospital, which has always tested the boundaries of what is medically possible at the same time as reaching out to the impoverished community it served. Thomas John Barnardo studied to be a doctor here before establishing what would be the first of his Dr Barnardo's orphanages for destitute children in 1870. In 1873 the hospital opened a School of Nursing, based on the principles of hygiene and organization championed by Florence Nightingale, and which from 1880 was run by her protégée, Eva Lückes, whom Frederick Treves described as 'one of the ablest and most remarkable women of the age'.

By the end of the nineteenth century it was the largest charitably funded hospital in Britain, with more than 1,000 beds, and it retained its independent charitable status and philanthropic ethos until the creation of the National Health Service in 1948. The fabric of the original complex had been much adapted over the years, but by 2012 the old buildings were no longer considered fit for the purpose of a twenty-first-century inner-city hospital. The new hospital, which rose like a phoenix behind it, remains in the vanguard of best medical practice.

So I shut the door on the past and left the old place. Soon it will be a centre of local government, serving the community in a different way. I hope the new occupants erect an appropriate memorial to the doctors, nurses and staff who made this such a special hospital over so many years. And I trust those who work here and visit will spare them a thought for they – we – have all benefited from the pioneering work carried out under this roof.

My investigations, however, were not quite over. Having spent so long in the past, I took a trip into the twenty-first century – in the lift that transported me to the roof of the new Royal London Hospital. The view from up here rivals any in the capital – west to the shimmering skyscrapers of the City, east to the blue haze of the Thames estuary and the North Sea beyond. A windsock was flying, billowed out by a brisk south-westerly. And below it sat the symbol of the new hospital – a red MD902 Explorer helicopter with yellow and green flashes that indicate its role as an emergency vehicle.

This was one of the two choppers of the London Air Ambulance fleet, formed in 1989 and based on the top of the original London Hospital until 2012, when it switched to the roof of the new building. The air ambulances are crewed with an advanced trauma doctor and a paramedic who are capable of performing life-saving operations, including open-heart surgery, at the scenes of accidents. Whizzing above London's congested streets, where the average traffic speed is 9 mph, they are capable of reaching 10 million people in an area of 600 square miles in just twelve minutes. This means they can attend to patients well within the crucial 'golden hour' when treatment is most likely to be effective.

We're talking fine margins here. On 16 April 1999, a twenty-two-year-old man from east London was knifed through the heart in the Swan pub in Stratford. One of the two men who now strode forward to greet me took up the story. 'We got a call: "There's a stabbing in a pub,"' said Alastair Mulcahy, a consultant anaesthetist at the Royal London and a trauma doctor on the Air Ambulance team. The victim was the man standing alongside him, Stephen Niland, who grinned ruefully.

When medics found Stephen slumped and losing lots of blood they knew it wasn't just a question of stabilizing him and flying him back to the hospital for emergency care. They had to act swiftly and bravely, on the spot. Alastair and his colleague each took a pair of scissors and cut through Stephen's chest from either side, meeting at the sternum. When they opened up the cavity they saw that the heart had stopped beating: 'Then a jet of blood came out,' said Alastair. Stephen's grin froze at this point in the story. He may have heard and recounted it a million times, but no one likes to remember how close they came to death.

Stephen's heart had been penetrated by the knife, so Alastair did the only thing he could do in the circumstances. He stuck his finger in the hole to stem the blood. He swiped up a photograph on his tablet, of an open and bloody chest cavity. 'Here's Stephen with his chest open. There's my hand with my finger in his heart.' We gathered round the screen, squinting in the sunlight. It's an image that sums up the 250-year history of the London Hospital, whose staff have never been afraid to take risks nor to push the boundaries of what's possible. Saving lives, in this most chaotic and vibrant of neighbourhoods, has depended on it.

Above: The grim precincts of Shepton Mallet prison today. When it was decommissioned in 2013 it was the country's oldest gaol, having been in continuous use for nearly 400 years.

Below: In 1944 a black GI, Leroy Henry, was sentenced to death at Shepton Mallet for the rape of a white woman. His case became a *cause célèbre*.

Below: A petition signed by thousands urged a review of his conviction, and General Eisenhower stepped in to revoke Henry's death sentence and exonerate him.

BATH WEEKLY CHRONICLE AND

eath Sentence for Attack On Bath Woman

COURT-MARTIAL ON COLOURED SOLDIER

held a knife over me," declared a Combe Down woman at a court martial at a United States Army p in the West Country on Thursday, when a coloured er was found guilty of rape and sentenced to be ed.

e Court included one red member. Captain ison prosecuted, and r Drew defended the ed, who pleaded not y. A colonel presided the Court, which con- d of eight officers.

woman said: "I am a house- don't know the accused

the Avenue heard someone coming at speed. He found it was his wife. Witness said: "I said, 'What- ever is the matter?' My wife said: 'Oh, he has got a knife.' I said: 'Where is he?' as I wanted to make after him. My wife said: 'Don't go. He will stab you with that knife.

" She said the man had assaulted her. She was nearly collapsing, so he took her to the Aid Post."

On the way to see the doctor his

20,000 PETITION EISENHOWER TO SAVE U.S. SOLDIER'S LIFE

Twenty thousand people have signed a petition sent to General Eisenhower from Bath on behalf of an American coloured soldier sentenced to death by court-martial for an offence against a Combe Down, Bath, woman.

Mrs. Mavis Tate, M.P. for Frome, has handed the Home Secretary a letter from a Trow- bridge woman worker urging that the soldier should have the chance to produce further evi- dence.

Many Trowbridge people have signed the reprieve petition

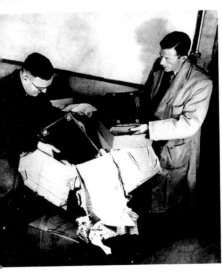

Above: Some of Shepton Mallet's most famous 'inmates' were not felons at all, but documents from the National Archives, sent here for safekeeping in World War Two. They included the logs of HMS *Victory* and, seen here, the Domesday Book (*left*) and Magna Carta (*right*).

Below: In 1952 Ronnie and Reggie Kray were a couple of jack-the-lads from London's East End with a few pro boxing fights under their belts. Their time at Shepton Mallet set them on a path of career criminality.

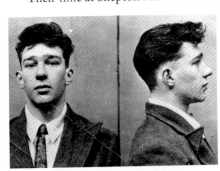

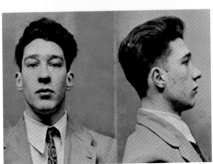

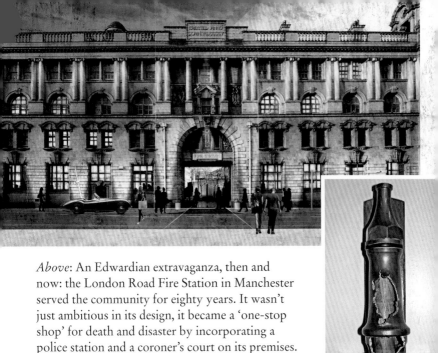

Above: An Edwardian extravaganza, then and now: the London Road Fire Station in Manchester served the community for eighty years. It wasn't just ambitious in its design, it became a 'one-stop shop' for death and disaster by incorporating a police station and a coroner's court on its premises.

Right: The damaged branch pipe held by Roy Skelton and William Varah, who lost their lives in the 'Christmas Blitz' of 1940. Thirty Manchester firefighters were killed in the war.

Below: Female operators in the control room, 1950. One of their unofficial roles was to be good listeners to the firemen who returned from distressing call-outs.

Above: Charles Booth's 'poverty map' of London from 1889, showing the most deprived areas in dark blue and black. The Royal London Hospital was in one of the poorest areas.

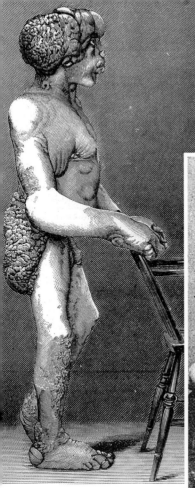

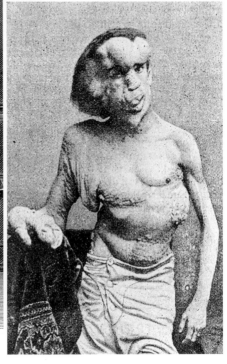

Left and below: Joseph Merrick, the Elephant Man, was exhibited by showman Tom Norman in a shop opposite the Royal London Hospital.

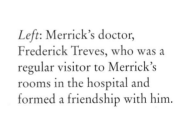

Left: Merrick's doctor, Frederick Treves, who was a regular visitor to Merrick's rooms in the hospital and formed a friendship with him.

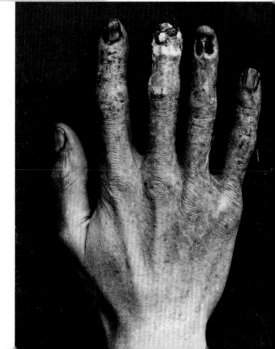

From hell

Mr Lusk

Sor I send you half the
Kidne I took from one women
prasarved it for you tother piece I
fried and ate it was very nise I
may send you the bloody knif that
took it out if you only wate a whil
longer.

Signed Catch me when
you Can
Mishter Lusk

Left: The infamous 'From Hell' letter, purporting to be from Jack the Ripper, which was sent to the chairman of the local vigilance committee, along with half a kidney. This was examined by Thomas Openshaw of the Royal London Hospital, who confirmed it was human. One of the Ripper's victims, Catherine Eddowes, had a kidney removed.

Right: The first X-ray machines were introduced at the Royal London Hospital in 1896. The results were groundbreaking but the dangers of radiation were not understood, which is why early radiographers were happy to use their hands as test objects. Four of them at the hospital lost their lives to radiation malignancy.

Above: The unabashed magnificence of Cambridge Military Hospital. Only the finest surroundings would do for the fighting forces of the mightiest nation on earth.

Left: In 1915, a young doctor called Harold Gillies persuaded the authorities to open a unit at the Cambridge dedicated to the treatment of soldiers' facial injuries. Here he performed miraculous feats of facial reconstruction. *Below*: The surgical room and specialist staff at the Cambridge Military Hospital.

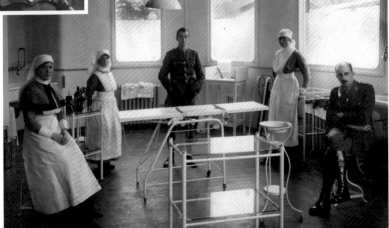

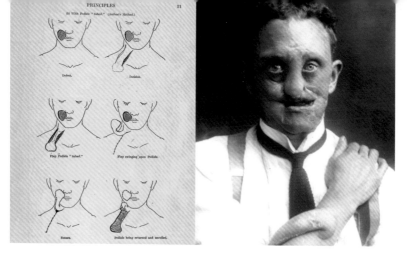

Above left: Harold Gillies pioneered the technique known as the 'tubed pedicle', a procedure that involved moving skin grafts stage by stage up to the patient's face. *Above right*: The tube-like graft is here attached to the patient's arm. The procedure of moving the graft was known as 'waltzing the pedicle' and could take many months.

Below left: Second World War Spitfire ace Robert Cowell, who became Roberta Cowell when Harold Gillies performed one of the first ever gender reassignment procedures from male to female. *Below right*: As Roberta Cowell she maintained her love of motor racing.

Cambridge Military Hospital, Aldershot

I was wearing a fur hat, walking through snow and approaching a palatial building fit for a czar. But I was nowhere near Russia. I was in the military town of Aldershot in Hampshire, regarded as the 'home of the British Army' since the establishment of the garrison in 1854. And the building was not a palace but a former hospital: Cambridge Military Hospital, which opened in 1879 and was named after the then Commander-in-Chief of the British Army, Prince George, Duke of Cambridge. It closed in 1996, due to high running costs and following the discovery of asbestos in the walls, and has been empty ever since.

The first thing that struck me was the sheer, unabashed grandeur of the place – a Victorian statement that nothing but the finest would do for the fighting forces of the mightiest nation on Earth. The yellow-brick façade is Italianate, with wings at each end. In the middle is a square tower with a belfry and clock turret commanding views of half of Hampshire and Surrey. It is indeed a magnificent monument, but not solely to the hegemony of the British military machine in the late nineteenth century. Something altogether more unexpected is memorialized in this fine old pile.

There are well-advanced plans to develop the site as a residential complex of flats and houses. But before the builders move in I was granted permission for one last look. More than two decades of dereliction have taken their toll, I was told. Ceilings are falling down, plaster is crumbling and paint is peeling. And many areas are out of bounds due to the presence of asbestos, which accounts for the 'Danger' and 'Do not enter' signs dotted about. But you'd hardly know it, looking from the outside. The old hospital maintains a dignified face – which is fitting considering that this is the place where men were once given new faces, new identities, after being robbed of both through the ravages of war.

Cambridge Military Hospital was the birthplace of reconstructive surgery in Britain – and has an extraordinary story with ramifications that echo to this day. But it started life with altogether more modest aims. It simply wanted to stem the horrendous haemorrhaging of lives among British soldiers wounded in action. To learn more, I enlisted the help of a man who has himself patched up wounds on the field of battle. Pete Starling is a former member of the Royal Army Medical Corps, who is now a military historian with a special interest in this hospital.

As we unlocked the front door and tiptoed among debris that has accumulated over the last twenty years, he pointed out that there is, after all, a Russian connection: the hospital was conceived in answer to questions raised by the Crimean War of 1853–6. This conflict between Russia and Allied forces from Britain, France, Sardinia and Turkey is perhaps remembered chiefly through its association with Florence Nightingale and Alfred, Lord Tennyson's narrative poem 'The Charge of the Light Brigade' ('Into the valley of Death/Rode the six hundred'), which was about the Battle of Balaclava in 1854. But as Pete told me, it was also significant as 'a war that changed the way armies fought and survived war'.

The Crimean War was the first war of the modern era. 'It was starting to get more industrialized,' said Pete. 'The warships were steam-powered. We had railways to carry supplies forward. We had photographers and war correspondents. They were able to get their stories and pictures back. And you could say that that was the problem.' Due to reports from the front line, the families of serving soldiers and the wider public became aware for the first time of the true nature of life at the sharp end of war – in particular the fact that many more men were dying from diseases such as cholera than from battle wounds.

In response, the social reformer Florence Nightingale took a team of volunteer nurses to the British military hospital at Scutari in Istanbul, to which casualties were evacuated across the Black Sea. Shocked by the conditions she found, she instigated a new regime based on improved hygiene practices, better ventilation, proper sewers and a decent diet. And in the aftermath of the war she campaigned for lessons to be learned. 'She'd got a lot of friends in high places in the Army and the government, so she was very influential,' said Pete.

Nightingale's exhaustive report on the limitations of medical care in the Crimean War formed the basis of a Royal Commission on the Health of the Army, which concluded that proper military hospitals should be built for our casualties of war. One of the first was the Herbert Hospital, which opened in Woolwich, south-east London, in 1865 and was named after Sidney Herbert, the politician who had sent Florence Nightingale to the Crimea. The Cambridge Hospital in Aldershot followed fourteen years later.

Both were designed on what Pete described as the Nightingale Plan: 'A big, long, central corridor. Big wards. Plenty of space for the beds.' We had now reached that central corridor and I paused to look up and down its rather dismaying length – measuring 528 feet, apparently. I knew this because Pete had brought along the original architect's drawings, which we unfurled and held up against the peeling wall.

There was the central spine of the corridor and, coming off it at right angles, wards on both of the two floors, each with six large sash windows on either side. We walked along a few paces, took the first door on the right and stepped into a large room, where the air swirled with the dust we had dislodged with our feet. There were lines of windows on each side, the lower halves boarded up and some of the upper panes cracked or smashed. 'Here you see an example of one of the big, high-ceilinged wards,' said Pete. 'Big windows. Plenty of light. Plenty of fresh air.'

When these wards were built no one could have envisaged the pressure they would be put under, the sheer volume of human suffering that would pass through them. The beds are long gone, of course. But now, as we stood there, we saw them in our mind's eye, we saw them filling up with the terrible harvest of the Great War of 1914–18.

On 23 August 1914, British forces were engaged for the first time in the First World War at the Battle of Mons. It was also their first engagement on European soil since the Crimean War. Within hours the wounded were evacuated by ship across the English Channel to Southampton, and then on to Cambridge Military Hospital, which became the first army-base hospital in history to receive casualties directly from the battle front. But as the casualties mounted on the Western Front, the military authorities realized they would have to grade and prioritize the wounded.

Pete invited me to picture our surroundings as a shattered chateau (not so hard, actually), somewhere behind the front lines of the fighting. 'If you can imagine I'm taking you into a ruined French building where we've got our dressing station, we can talk about triage, which means "to sort" – how we would prioritize our casualties. A man has a head wound. He doesn't look too good. If it's a penetrating wound of his skull his chances of survival are not that great. We don't want to waste too much time on him.' The reality was that he was allowed to die so that six or seven others could be saved. Such is the cruel reckoning of war.

Casualties with minor wounds were recycled back into front-line fighting. Those with more serious injuries were shipped back to England. In military parlance they were suffering from 'Blighty wounds', i.e. wounds severe enough to require prolonged treatment in a proper hospital at home. From 1915 the wards of Cambridge Military Hospital filled up with such men. In previous wars many may not have survived. But improved medical practice along the whole chain of rescue and care – from the stretcher-bearers who picked up the wounded in no man's land to the hospitals back in Blighty – saved many lives.

There was, however, an unforeseen consequence. Yes, men were surviving – but many had sustained injuries that left them unrecognizable. It is estimated that more than 20 million soldiers, on both sides of the conflict, were wounded in the First World War. The weapons deployed on the Western Front brought death and destruction on an industrialized scale. Artillery shells – filled with shrapnel to cause maximum damage – machine guns and poison gas all created injuries never seen before. A single bullet from a standard-issue infantryman's rifle, such as the .303 calibre Lee–Enfield used by the British Army, could leave an exit wound up to twenty times bigger than the entry wound.

The trench warfare that characterized the First World War made men's faces particularly vulnerable as they risked being hit by a sniper's bullet every time they took a peek over the top. In 1915 a young New Zealand doctor called Harold Gillies noted the high incidence of facial injuries while he was serving on the Western Front with the Red Cross. The Army had already established Queen Mary's Hospital, Roehampton, as a specialist centre for amputees. Gillies now persuaded the authorities to sanction a unit in Aldershot dedicated to the treatment of facial injuries. Here, and later at Queen Mary's Hospital in Sidcup, Kent, he was to perform miraculous feats of facial reconstruction.

My next interviewee, Andrew Bamji, is a retired consultant in rheumatology and rehabilitation, and has worked and written extensively on facial injury. He approached me down the long corridor carrying a cardboard box and, he said, feeling humbled to be walking, literally, in the footsteps of Harold Gillies.

'Harold started from nothing and developed techniques for mending the face that had never been done before,' Andrew told me. 'He's really the father of plastic surgery.' He showed me a photograph of Gillies in his Army uniform, taken near the beginning of the First World War. He is balding and slight and, said Andrew, 'doesn't look particularly prepossessing, but he is only thirty-three'. Gillies assembled around him a team of physicians, dentists, photographers, artists and specialist nurses. His early efforts were confined to cosmetic masks, which is where Andrew's box came in.

Opening it carefully, he lifted from the tissue-paper wrapping a pair of old-fashioned round glasses with a flesh-coloured tin panel attached. 'What we can see here is a missing cheek, attached to a little bridge over the nose and a pair of spectacles,' he said. 'It's a very, very thin plate, and painted quite nicely to match [the patient's face], with a *slight* variation of colour under the eye, which would fit with the crease under the eye that most people have.'

It was an exquisitely crafted, strangely moving object – to think that a maimed survivor of that war of mechanized slaughter had worn this to save face and spare other people the sight of his terrible disfigurement. Andrew showed me another example of Gillies' cosmetic masks in the form of 'before' and 'after' photographs of a man who had lost an eye. 'In this case the patient has had a pair of glasses made with a face mask that contains a glass eye,' he explained. 'The eyelids are nicely made up, probably with silver wire for the eyelashes.'

Well intentioned and cleverly constructed as they were, these masks were soon superseded by an altogether more ambitious approach to facial injury. 'Gillies moved away from trying to cover up a hole,' said Andrew. 'Structure is not the only thing that's important. Function is also important. The problem with the masks, Harold Gillies found, was that patients didn't like them. They were cold, they were unemotional, they were actually extremely uncomfortable very often.'

How, indeed, would I like to walk around with a piece of painted tin covering half my face? What Gillies intended was not merely to disguise facial disfigurement. He meant to mend it, using living tissue. It's only now that I was beginning to appreciate the enormity of Gillies' work in these now-derelict wards. He was not just performing groundbreaking surgical procedures, but was trying to make broken men whole again, to give them back their sense of self.

Our faces are our identity. Each day we see ourselves in the mirror and look for that reassuring symmetry. We smile, we frown, we wink. But what happens when we lose that symmetry, that familiar face, due to catastrophic damage? With a face changed beyond recognition, who are we? It's a profound philosophical question and in the midst of the most destructive conflict in world history, Gillies wasn't afraid to ask it, or to try to answer it.

To understand the complexities of the surgery Gillies pioneered I turned to Colonel Alan Kay, a consultant plastic surgeon who specializes in trauma reconstruction and has served with the British Army in Iraq and Afghanistan. He joined me in one of the wards in which Gillies would have worked. 'The sorts of injuries he ended up dealing with were cases with large amounts of tissue missing – the nose, half the jaw, part of the skull,' Colonel Kay said. 'These sorts of injuries were historically unreconstructable.'

At this time reconstructive surgeons were severely limited in what they could do. Wounds too big to be stitched up could be patched with a simple 'split' skin graft from a donor site such as the thigh – 'split' meaning that the graft consists of the top layer of skin, the epidermis, but only half the layer beneath, the dermis. 'But the trouble with the split skin graft is that wounds will always try to make themselves smaller,' explained Colonel

Kay. 'Over a period of time it will contract and you will cause another deformity.'

An alternative, he said, would be to use a graft of the full thickness of the skin as that will not contract in the same way: 'In terms of appearance it's far superior. The trouble is, where you've got more complex reconstructions it's not going to pick up enough blood supply and it will die.' The challenge for Gillies was to somehow keep the flesh alive as he attempted to graft it from one part of the body to the damaged facial area.

His solution was to develop a technique known as the 'tubed pedicle' – a procedure so bizarre, to this layman at least, that it seems scarcely credible for it to have been tried in the first place, or that it worked in the second. It was, as is often the case in scientific breakthroughs, a case of accidental discovery. Gillies had been presented with a patient, Able Seaman Willie Vicarage, whose face had been badly burned at the Battle of Jutland, the largest naval battle of the war, on 1 June 1916.

Gillies set about taking grafts from the man's chest and noticed that when he lifted a flap of skin it naturally formed a tube shape, and that this reduced the risk of infection to the raw areas and improved the blood supply. Rather than cut the skin flap entirely free, he decided to maintain the connection at one end to keep the blood flowing through the graft while moving the other end.

'But now we've got to get this tissue up to here,' said Colonel Kay, pointing at his face. 'It's not going to get up to there in a single go. We've got to go through an intermediary.

And what was commonly used in Gillies' time was the patient's arm.' I was not sure I was understanding this correctly, so Andrew Bamji showed me photographs, part of Gillies' exhaustive and meticulous record of his pioneering work in plastic surgery.

Men with holes in their faces stared back as if defying me to look away, for their heads, shoulders and arms were covered in bizarre, trunk-like growths that showed the skin graft in transit, as it were, from the donor site to the face wound. These 'tubed pedicles' and the procedure of moving them in stages could take many months. 'The term that was adopted was "waltzing",' said Colonel Kay. 'They would "waltz" the pedicle.'

By this improbable but brilliantly conceived technique, Gillies performed near-miracles, returning to many men their identities and self-respect when they had given up hope of ever recovering either. 'Men without half their faces; men burned and maimed to the condition of animals. Day after day, the tragic grotesque procession disembarked from the hospital ships and made its way towards us,' wrote Gillies, recalling those days at Aldershot and Sidcup.

There were failures, notably the case of Henry Ralph Lumley of the Royal Flying Corps who crash-landed his plane on his first solo flight in 1917 and sustained horrific burns to the face. Gillies' attempt to replace the skin of Lumley's face with a skin graft from the chest went horribly wrong when the flesh became gangrenous. Sadly, Lumley died in 1918. But Willie Vicarage, the badly burned seaman, came through.

Andrew showed me a sequence of photographs showing Vicarage's progress from a man without nose or lips to a chap who just looked as if he'd been in a bit of a punch-up. In between was a picture of tubed pedicles, having been cut from the chest, growing up from either shoulder to the middle of his face. 'This triangular flap has been raised from the chest and he is the first British tubed pedicle ever done,' said Andrew. 'It was successful. You can see from the end result there that he got quite a reasonable appearance.'

I had heard of Harold Gillies but was only vaguely aware of what he achieved. It is no surprise to discover that he was knighted (somewhat belatedly) in 1930 for his medical achievements and services in the First World War. But he was not a man to rest on his laurels, or to devote the rest of his life to his favourite pastime of golf (at which, it was no surprise to hear, he excelled). The avenues he chose to explore in later life did not just extend the boundaries of medicine, however. They tested society's morals and hovered on the edge of what was legal.

Before I learned about this extraordinary period of his life I wanted to know more about the experience of the patient who underwent the kind of radical medical procedures in which he specialized. For Gillies, I'm sure, would have been the first to admit that his achievements would not have been possible without the co-operation and bravery of the men who submitted to his scalpel.

Of course, none of Gillies' patients is still alive. But there is someone who provides a direct link to the great man. His name is Doug Vince, he's ninety-five years old and he was now striding towards me along that long corridor with a spring in his step. In 1945, he explained, he received reconstructive surgery from Gillies' cousin and protégé Archibald McIndoe, who became famous in his own right as a plastic surgeon during and after the Second World War.

At the outbreak of the war McIndoe was assigned to Queen Victoria Hospital in East Grinstead, which specialized in burns injuries sustained by RAF aircrew. In 1945 Doug Vince was a twenty-two-year-old flight engineer on Stirling bombers. His plane came under attack from an enemy aircraft as it returned from a sortie over Germany. 'A German fighter came back with us as we flew at night. He shot at us and set the plane on fire. And I passed out because of the smoke,' he recalled.

'When the pilot landed, the aircraft was in flames. I came round and saw a square of moonlight. I remember thinking, "I can live!" I clambered out of the escape hatch and ran along the wing. I thought it might explode as it was burning quite furiously. I was still running when I went off the end.' His face and both hands were burned. His hands required reconstructive work, which McIndoe carried out at Queen Victoria Hospital.

'They grafted my hands,' said Doug, turning over his right hand and flexing the fingers of his left. The skin was a little paler and smoother, but you'd hardly have known he'd been in such a terrible situation. The skin, he said, came from his leg and stomach, and the grafts were straightforward. But it wasn't just the physical repair I was interested in. That, if you'll pardon the pun, was just skin-deep. Doug had a more significant story to tell and the tie he was wearing was a way into it. The tie was maroon-coloured, with blue and white stripes and an odd little repeat motif. 'A tiny guinea pig with wings,' he confirmed. This is the tie of the Guinea Pig Club, an exclusive group that is growing more exclusive by the year. 'Out of six hundred and forty-something of us at the end of war, when we last met there were just six of us,' he said.

The club was founded in the summer of 1941 at East Grinstead and membership was confined to members of the RAF who had had surgery at Queen Victoria Hospital and the surgeons who had operated on them. It wasn't McIndoe's idea apparently, but he went along with it enthusiastically. On one level it was just a bit of fun – the barrel of beer that became a permanent fixture on one of the wards was a sure-fire winner among the recovering young men.

But there was a more serious purpose. For, as McIndoe said, 'It is one thing to cure the patient of his disfigurement and deformity, it is another to carry through such an arduous programme and end up with a normal human being.' McIndoe was ahead of his time in regarding medical treatment in what nowadays might be called a 'holistic' way. Like his cousin Harold Gillies, he considered the lasting psychological effects of disfigurement and the need for patients to feel confident of their own identity and normality. It is telling that Doug's most powerful memory of McIndoe is the moment he took his badly burned hand in his: 'He held it, and looked at it like it was something very valuable. He said, "I think we can help you." The three grafts made it nearly normal. I'm a lucky lad.'

In a sense, the next part of the story I was pursuing here was entirely logical. If a patient requires a physical fix, whether in wartime or peacetime, and a surgeon has the vision and expertise to provide it, should he not do so? My reaction would be to say 'Of course' – yet I was genuinely shocked and surprised to discover the later events of Harold Gillies' life.

In these now derelict spaces, where damaged men once felt the extremes of pain and elation, I arranged to meet a woman who knows of the extremes to which desperate men will go. Diana Cowell, an elegant and friendly woman in her early seventies, is the daughter of a Second World War Spitfire ace called Robert Cowell, who became a dashing racing driver in the post-war years. She showed me photographs of him in his RAF flying helmet and behind the wheel of a racing car. He was the very image of male vigour and 'normality'.

Diana has only vague memories of her father. For when she was four years old he left the family home to change his gender to female and she never saw him again. When she told me this I couldn't for the life of me square such facts with the apparently masculine man in the photographs. But Diana, who has spent a lifetime coming to terms with her father's behaviour, had a counter-intuitive explanation. 'That's probably why: "I am in a man's body therefore I must prove I am a man,"' she said.

The next part of the story struck me as even more shocking. For the surgeon who in 1951 facilitated Robert Cowell's sex change to enable him to become Roberta Cowell, thereby performing one of the first-ever gender-reassignment procedures from male to female, was Harold – by now *Sir* Harold – Gillies. 'He actually practised the night before on a cadaver because he'd never done the operation before. It had never been done in this country before,' Diana told me.

In 1954, Roberta Cowell sold her story to the periodical magazine *Picture Post* for £8,000 (at least £200,000 in today's money) and appeared on the front cover in a blue dress with a tumble of ginger-blonde curls. The shock of first losing her father, then discovering that 'he' was a woman, has affected Diana profoundly. 'I don't think I've ever got over it. I'm still very emotional about it because I will always have this little hurt child in my heart – "That's not my daddy, that's not my daddy!"'

There is a final, even more bizarre twist to this story. In a series of operations dating from 1946, Gillies had performed Britain's first-ever female-to-male sex change, using the tubed pedicle technique. His patient was Laura (later Michael) Dillon, a medical student at the time he transitioned. Dillon, who wrote a book about the predicament of being transgender, became friends with Robert/Roberta Cowell and agreed to help her out in her own gender journey. Cowell's problem was that she was still physically, and therefore legally, a man and it was illegal for a doctor to perform the surgical castration she required. Dillon obliged and this left Cowell free to approach Gillies for the vaginoplasty she needed to complete the change.

All this left me amazed, but not as shocked as I may have been a decade ago. Transgender and non-binary issues are just about the last taboo in terms of sexual identity. While homosexuality is now generally accepted by society, to the extent that legislation to allow same-sex marriages in the UK was passed in parliament in 2013, those who do not identify with the physical gender they were born with, or feel they are neither wholly masculine nor feminine but somewhere in between, have remained as fearful of expressing themselves as gay people once did.

But attitudes are slowly changing. As transgender and non-binary people are speaking out, mainstream opinion is catching up with what Gillies came to realize in Cambridge Military Hospital a century ago, that being comfortable in one's body is vital to a sense of equanimity and identity. As his sex-change patient Michael Dillon wrote, 'Where the mind cannot be made to fit the body, the body should be made to fit, approximately at any rate, to the mind.'

In visiting this hospital I uncovered a chain reaction of cause and effect that started with soldiers dying needlessly of disease in the Crimean War and concluded with gender-reassignment surgery. It was a bewildering journey, but it's an object lesson in how things change for the better – not, as we like to think, in an orderly and logical progression but through fate and chance, and the instincts of brilliant minds.

None was more brilliant than Harold Gillies. When I arrived outside Cambridge Military Hospital I saw it as a monument to a bygone age. It looked grand but bleak in the snow, entirely irrelevant to the modern era. But in leaving it I reflected that what happened here, and what it led to, points us firmly towards the future.

Brighton's Sewer System

This is a story of parallel cities, of equal and opposite worlds. Brighton, that rather ritzy resort on the south coast of England, means different things to different people: the onion-domed Brighton Pavilion and the excesses of the Regency period; the sleazy pre-war milieu of Graham Greene's 1938 novel *Brighton Rock*; the notably gay-friendly environment of the post-war years. I, for one, will always associate it with Conservative Party Conferences – one in particular, when five people were murdered and many others were seriously injured in a terrorist bomb attack on the Grand Hotel, very shortly after I had left it.

I shall address this terrible episode later in the book. For now I wish to explore a Brighton that few visitors pause to consider: the one beneath their feet, the one they can't see but would know about soon enough if it ceased to function. It may not be as grand-looking as the one up top, the Brighton of the aforementioned Pavilion, of cream stucco, ornate ironwork and glorious Regency squares. But it was actually better built because it had to be. The health of a rapidly expanding town depended on it, and still does.

This hidden Brighton is the system of sewers that processes the waste of its citizens and visitors. It is an aspect of public health that we take for granted now, but in mid-nineteenth-century Brighton it was a suitably bold and dramatic solution to a problem that was threatening to overwhelm the town. To understand the full extent and implications of that crisis I turned to an expert on Brighton's cultural history. Geoffrey Mead is a social geographer who grew up in Brighton, studied at the University of Sussex and now teaches there.

We met on the beach by the Palace Pier and strolled west, in silence at first as we absorbed the unique pleasures of being beside the seaside. 'I love walking along Brighton Beach,' he said. 'If you close your eyes and walk you've got water lapping at the stones, you've got the cry of the seagulls, and then you open your eyes and you're on the seashore of a large city, full of people enjoying themselves.'

Two hundred years ago, visitors to Brighton were not here just to have fun. They were on a mission to improve their health. A short time before, Brighton had been an obscure fishing village with the much less snappy name of Brighthelmstone. Its fortunes were turned around by a physician called Richard Russell, who cannily marketed what were essentially detox breaks for London's leisured upper classes. 'He starts to direct people down to property he owns on the coast, to the new "simple life" that you have in Brighthelmstone,' Geoff told me. 'It's about getting away from London. London is the most polluted spot on earth. When you come down to the seaside you are dipped in the sea, you get a wash, which not many rich people *did*. You're given seawater to drink, either neat or mixed with rum or porter, or, excruciatingly, with milk. Of course, seawater is an emetic and with the diet that the very rich had at that time – too much rich food and alcohol – making you sick is very good. You go back to London and people say, "Michael, you look exceedingly well!" To which you answer, "I've been to Brighthelmstone!" That's how it starts.'

In 1810 this rapidly expanding resort officially changed its name to the more user-friendly 'Brighton'. On 21 September 1841 the railway arrived in Brighton, slashing travelling time from the capital to less than two hours, and in the following decade the novelist William Makepeace Thackeray coined its most popular nickname when he referred to 'kind, cheerful, merry Doctor Brighton' in acknowledgement of its supposedly health-giving properties. The trouble was, a booming population – swelled by the seasonal influx of visitors – was turning the town into the very opposite of healthy.

Geoff took up the story again: 'There was no provision for sewage disposal. The authorities were relying on the fact that Brighton is built on a chalk landscape. You dig a hole in the chalk, pour liquid into it and the liquid disappears.' The question was, where did it disappear *to*? In 1849 an engineer called Edward Cresy produced the answer in a report to the General Board of Health 'into the sewerage, drainage, and supply of water, and the sanitary condition of the inhabitants of the town of Brighton'. Cresy pinpointed, as an example, one street of fifty-five houses which was served by two cesspits that were never emptied. 'Which isn't a major problem,' said Geoff, 'until you realize that they're on a steep hill, and the next street has its well immediately below that, and below that is another street with stables, and below that is another well. And so the entire water table is heavily polluted.'

Inadequate or non-existent sewage treatment, contaminated water supplies, poor sanitation and hygiene – all the conditions were in place for the spreading of waterborne and other diseases. The neighbourhoods where the poorest families lived, servicing the needs of the burgeoning middle class and health-conscious visitors, were particularly vulnerable. In 1849, the year of Cresy's damning report, Brighton suffered a virulent outbreak of cholera which claimed the lives of more than 200 people. The good doctors and burghers of Brighton, however, were conspicuously silent on the matter: to publicize the problem was to risk killing the goose that, even then, was laying the golden egg of health tourism.

It was left to *The Lancet*, the house journal of the medical profession, to campaign to alleviate the conditions in Brighton that made it particularly prone to outbreaks of cholera and diseases such as typhus and scarlet fever. To follow what happened next, I left Geoff Mead to his beloved beach and doubled back towards the Palace Pier before crossing the seafront road and walking away from the sea into Old Steine Gardens.

This is the former heart of the old fishing village of Brighthelmstone and the centre of Regency Brighton, a beautifully tended and landscaped park with the Royal Pavilion and Pavilion Gardens lying slightly to the north and west. It's a lovely spot in anyone's book but looked especially attractive on this cold but sunny late winter's day, with the promise of spring in the fresh sea air. However, I had no time for such a charming scene. I was seeking darkness, dankness and rank smells. I found them beneath a metal access hatch on the eastern side of the gardens.

Following reports in *The Lancet* on Brighton's health crisis, it became apparent that Dr Brighton badly needed a dose of his own medicine. It came in the form of a plan to build an extensive network of sewers in order to separate humans from their effluent. This was an age of radical reappraisal of the causes of disease and the preventative role of good hygiene and sanitation. As discussed in the previous chapter, Florence Nightingale based her new regime of hospital care on lessons learned in the Crimean War. In Soho, central London, Dr John Snow traced the source of a cholera epidemic to a single public water pump in the mid-1850s. For this he is credited with being the 'father' of epidemiology, the study of the incidence, distribution and possible control of diseases.

In Brighton the cause of cholera and other disease outbreaks was incontrovertible. Between 1869 and 1874, the town council spent over £100,000 (the equivalent of more than £6.5 million today) constructing a vast network of sewers to serve Britain's most popular seaside resort. The system included service and escape hatches at regular intervals and I was now hovering over one such hatch in Old Steine Gardens. I should point out, incidentally, that for my impending underground visit I had been togged out in a hard hat with head torch and gloves.

A steel ladder took me down into the bowels of Dr Brighton. It was unpleasant down there of course – humid, nasty and smelly, though the odour wasn't nearly as bad as I had feared and I ceased to notice it after a while – but it was also magnificent in its own way, for this is a typically ambitious Victorian concept brilliantly realized by superb engineering work. Over five years of construction, millions of tons of earth were removed, not by mechanical diggers but by the sweat of labourers using picks and shovels. The resulting tunnels were braced with timbers and lined with an estimated 7 million bricks, every single one laid with skill and precision. The cross-section of the tunnels was egg-shaped rather than round, as the sewage was propelled not by pumps but by gravity and the shallow V-shape maximized the flow.

I squelched my way south (or possibly north) to a constant soundtrack of rushing water with my head torch sending light and shadows dancing along the walls. The dead roots of vegetation penetrated the vaulted brick roof. White salt crystals dusted the brick walls. The rush of water grew louder and deeper till it sounded as if the ocean itself were no further than an arm's length away and I found myself in a large chamber – the place

I had arranged to meet my next witness, Stuart Slark. He is an engineer with Southern Water, the water authority in charge of maintaining Brighton's sewer network, and is intimately familiar with the labyrinth of tunnels.

We shook gloved hands and paused to consider our surroundings. As torchlight illuminated the brick roof, the chamber looked to be the size of an old railway station. 'The Victorians always thought big and built large,' said Stuart. 'The tank we're in now is an overflow chamber. On the right-hand side over there, where I'm shining my torch, on the other side of that wall is a foul sewer. If we have heavy rain it'll come down that foul sewer and over that wall to where we're standing now.' These Victorian tunnels and chambers still provide the backbone of Brighton's modern sewerage system, disposing of 22 million gallons of waste water on an average day. That figure rises to 90 million on a day of storms and heavy rain. When the foul sewers overflow, this chamber fills up in no time. If I were here when it happened, would I be able to escape? One thing is for certain, it would not be a pleasant way to go.

There are some 44 miles of sewage tunnels beneath Brighton that are either walkable or navigable by boat. 'But there are so many arteries, veins and lead-offs, I don't know how they ever managed to do it,' said Stuart. It's the precision of the engineering work that impresses him every time he comes down here: 'This is the incredible thing.'

As he led me back through a twisting safety tunnel another thought struck me. I had only the vaguest idea of where we were in relation to Brighton's street pattern, under which square or roundabout we may have been making our way. But suppose, for a moment, that we were directly underneath one of the town's architectural showpieces, one of those seafront Regency terraces painted the colour of clotted cream, with capitals, architraves and other classical embellishments. As undeniably magnificent as they look, they are something of an illusion. The splendour of the façades often hides shoddy workmanship behind. This, in Graham Greene's phrase, is 'the shabby secret behind the bright corsage' for many of Brighton's Regency houses were built using a cheap and inferior material known as 'bungaroush', a mix of lime and flint and anything else that came to hand.

Bungaroush is notably porous and would never have done for Brighton's sewers, which were built to last by skilled engineers and bricklayers using the finest materials. The truth is that the hidden city I was now exploring was constructed to higher standards than the one up top. When I climbed the steel ladder to emerge back in that world of sunlight and seagulls, it looked different, gaudy and complacent. But they are, of course, flip sides of the same coin. One would not exist without the other. In the space of thirty years in the mid-nineteenth century, railways, pleasure piers, grand hotels and, yes, sewers combined to usher in the golden age of the British seaside. It was, across the piece, a triumph of Victorian ingenuity.

PART III

Defence of the Realm

The highlight of my political career? That's an easy question to answer. It was the period I served as the Secretary of State for Defence, between 1995 and 1997. This wasn't so much because I occupied one of the highest political offices, though I was certainly proud on that score. It was mainly to do with the people I dealt with. Some were civil servants, many were in the military. All were high-grade individuals – intellectually rigorous with tremendous personal qualities of bravery, enthusiasm, commitment and, in most cases, personal loyalty. So it was an absolute pleasure to run into such types again while visiting the sites and developing the themes of this section on the 'Defence of the Realm'.

I was also reminded of how little I knew, *really* knew, despite supposedly being all-seeing and all-knowing as Defence Secretary. Of course, I was made aware of current secret research and covert operations but that was usually on a 'need to know' basis, because they required my authority or funding. On my first day in the defence job I wasn't presented with a dossier listing all the highly classified activities in which the government and the military were engaged, and I rather doubt that the prime minister was either.

This is how the world of state secrecy operates, by ensuring that not too much information is accumulated in a single place or a single mind. That applied to me, as Defence Secretary, and also to a person such as twenty-two-year-old Roger Darlington in 1971, when he was pitched into the top-secret world of Cold War espionage alongside tight-lipped American spooks. This was at Cobra Mist, a hush-hush installation on the Suffolk coast patrolled by military police with big dogs and even bigger guns. Roger was a technician responsible for processing highly classified data but, having signed the Official Secrets Act, he thought it safest to say he was just a cleaner when quizzed by curious locals in the village pub.

Cobra Mist was just one among a plethora of secret sites located in a remote spot called Orford Ness, well away from the public gaze. The various research and development projects that took place there closed down well before I joined the government, so although I had heard of Orford Ness I didn't appreciate just how vital it had been to the defence of the realm. Many innovations, great and small, were tested and perfected in these windswept huts and labs, by men and women who perfectly fitted the epithet 'boffin'.

They were scientists, academics, engineers and military personnel, and they had a genius for applying their field of expertise to defence and military imperatives – characters such as Professor John Allen, now ninety-five and one of the last of his generation, who tracked the flight paths of dummy nuclear bombs as they were dropped over East Anglia (he admitted that at least one landed in someone's back garden). For the most part this vital work wasn't glamorous. It did not yield instant results but proceeded painstakingly, by trial and (frequently dangerous) error. The real revelation, for me, was just how dangerous it was on occasion. I knew that nuclear weapons had been tested on Orford Ness but the official line has always been that there was never any chance of a catastrophic accident. One of my witnesses, a man who stress-tested nuclear bombs, told another story.

His admission shocked me but I reflected later that it wasn't so surprising. In military research, as in civilian life, strategies and policies are often riddled with holes. The fate of Imber, the little village on Salisbury Plain that fell victim to Britain's mighty war machine, is a brew of cock-up and conspiracy – in what proportions no one can be sure. I had been there before, again in my capacity as Defence Secretary, but the village had made a negligible impression on me. It was a training area, nothing more. I had no idea of the continuities that had been broken, the families disrupted, by what happened here at the end of 1943. The irony is that Imber embodied, in its longevity and peacefulness, the very qualities we went to war to protect. On my return, I was engulfed not just by the story, but by the spirit of the place – forlorn, yes, but not quite extinguished. It lives on in fragments of buildings, in the church especially, and in the old Imber families who walked its ghostly streets with me.

If Imber moved me, the nuclear bunker in Cambridge left me perturbed. From the early 1950s right through to the end of the Cold War, it was assigned a vital role in our civil defence strategy as a Regional Seat of Government (RSG) – a sort of mini-Whitehall – should Britain suffer nuclear attack by the Soviet Union. When the country was laid waste by radioactive fallout and physical destruction on an unimaginable scale, it was the chaps in the RSGs who would keep our peckers up by broadcasting reassuring news, playing stirring songs, and plying us with biscuits.

The idea was absurd, the planning farcical. The story of the RSGs would have been funny if it hadn't been so serious. For while bewildered personnel on war exercises were wandering through provincial towns asking for directions to the local top-secret bunker, the Cold War was hotting up. It reached boiling point with the Cuban Missile Crisis of 1962. It was fascinating for me to revisit this seminal episode in twentieth-century history. Though I remember it, I didn't *understand* it and felt the enormity of it principally through the reactions of my parents. Here, I was able to meet people who were there, at the sharp end of history.

One was a crew member of a nuclear-armed British bomber on just a few minutes' notice to attack the Soviet Union. As the bombers stood at attack-readiness on the runway, he advised his wife to jump in the car and drive to the Isle of Skye. 'I think you'll be safe there,' he told her. Meanwhile, he contemplated a mission from which he almost certainly would not have returned. Some 4,000 miles away the commander of a Soviet submarine was caught in America's naval blockade of Cuba. Hiding far beneath the surface, out of radio contact, he heard explosions and did not know whether the Third World War had started – and, if it had, how to react. 'The situation was very difficult,' he told me, with considerable understatement.

Such testimonies were priceless and validated the whole approach of *Portillo's Hidden History of Britain* in getting people who were there to tell it how it was. For this section, in particular, I met a great many people and in some cases they were individuals I would almost certainly never have encountered as Defence Secretary. The Soviet submariner was one; Beth, a former Greenham Common peace campaigner, another. In 1988 she 'invaded' Imber as part of an anti-war protest that was quasi-military in its audacity, planning and element of surprise. I didn't have to agree with her world view to appreciate her testimony, or her sincerity.

In the end, though, it was meeting and hearing about the unsung heroes of the British defence establishment that will stick in my mind. To get back to my original point, they were solid, dependable types who, at the most basic level, turned up on time and did what they said they would do. They weren't warmongers – indeed, they often tended towards caution –

but they were enthusiastic for new approaches when it looked as if the old ones weren't working. They had a can-do spirit. And it was that spirit that got us through, when the dark ages threatened to return.

Imber Village, Wiltshire

On 7 February 1996, when I was Secretary of State for Defence, I went to the Salisbury Plain Training Area in Wiltshire to observe the British Army on exercise. The exercise in question was called 'Phantom Bugle' and it tested the mettle of the Army's tanks and armoured vehicles, supported by troops and aircraft, in a simulated battle environment. I remember sitting in a Warrior fighting vehicle and hearing the rumble of military hardware moving at speed over the battle-scarred terrain and the clatter of blank ammunition being fired. And I was dimly aware, at one point, of a group of buildings, the spectral outlines of a village in the midst of all this noise and movement. But I had no idea of the poignancy of the story hidden within its shell-shattered walls.

The name of this ghost village is Imber. More than twenty years later I returned, this time with my eyes open, to find a main street littered with spent cartridges, grenade pins and bullet clips, and lined with pockmarked buildings. Merely getting here was no mean feat, for Imber now occupies the most physically dangerous spot in the United Kingdom. The road in from the nearest town, Warminster, was lined with warning signs such as 'Danger. Unexploded Military Debris' and 'Do Not Leave the Carriageway', and the surrounding plain was dotted with the hulks of tanks that now serve as target practice. For this is the largest military training area in the realm, with a rugged terrain that is ideal for the testing of tanks and the training of their crews, and Imber is in the heart of it, which explains why it is off-limits to the general public for all but a handful of designated days a year. This limitation dictated the scope of my investigations. I had to get in and out in a few hours. The meetings I arranged, with people who I trusted to unlock Imber's secrets, had to be conducted with military precision and punctuality.

First impressions were of a dead place. Houses stripped of adornment, windows or gardens, and capped with metal roofs. A cluster of buildings that some people apparently refer to as 'Legoland' but reminded me of the green houses and red hotels in the Monopoly board game. There were weeds everywhere. The one structure still intact was a Norman church – oddly, I didn't recall that from 1996 – set back from the main street on rising ground. Birds sang but in a wistful register, or so it seemed to me.

It felt as if the spirit of this sad, abandoned place had drained away long ago. But this is not quite true – a fellowship of people keep it alive and they are the ones I was relying on to lead me through its history. It is a story about a village with deep roots whose inhabitants were uprooted, ignored and 'betrayed' – all in the name of a greater freedom. One of the people I met is the only person still alive who witnessed the crucial moment in its apparent betrayal. His name is John Williams and we talked outside the old schoolhouse – down from the church, on the edge of 'Legoland' – where it happened. We'll come to John, and all the others who believed their lives were altered by a broken promise. On my return to Salisbury Plain I was determined to pay Imber the attention and respect that too many in authority failed to show it over the decades.

If you look at the village on a map you will see it marooned amid the desolate tracts of the western part of Salisbury Plain. A local rhyme sums it up: 'Imber on the down/Seven miles from any town'. The roads to it from the relative civilization of the nearest villages were once narrow and turfed. Now they are scored with caterpillar tracks and dotted with those broken tanks. The Salisbury Plain Training Area is a secure zone where the Army can fire live ammunition and drive tanks at combat speed on exercises designed to replicate the kind of battle conditions they may be expected to encounter in different theatres of conflict.

The training area occupies half of the plain, which is otherwise notable for its wealth of ancient archaeology. The circle of standing stones at Stonehenge is just the most famous of sites that also include Iron Age hill forts, Bronze Age settlements and Neolithic burial mounds. More recently, the Anglo-Saxons established farmsteads on and around the plain, which has been inhabited and farmed for many centuries.

Imber is nearly as old as the chalk hills that surround it. It appeared in a Saxon charter of AD 967 and in 1086 was recorded in the Domesday Book, the survey of land ownership and tax obligations in England and Wales ordered by William the Conqueror. 'Imemerie', as it was then spelled, is noted as being 'quite small', with just seven households, two 'ploughlands' and three 'pastures' – and a negligible taxable value of just '2 geld units'. It was never to be a place of any significance or influence. By the mid-twelfth century it had a church, replaced in the thirteenth and fourteenth centuries by the present building, dedicated to St Giles, which has traces of medieval paintings on its walls.

Imber's population peaked in the mid-nineteenth century at about 450. In the 1890s the Wiltshire writer Ella Noyes described it as 'one straggling street of old cottages and farmsteads winding along the hollow under the sheltering elms'. Set back at one end of that 'straggling street' was the church, with the manor house, Imber Court, at the other. In between was a pub, a Baptist chapel, a schoolhouse and a blacksmith. This was the spirit of old England made manifest.

By the outbreak of the Second World War the population had dropped to some 150 people, but Imber remained a sleepy, self-contained community with a way of life essentially unchanged in centuries. Poking around in the weed-bound shell of an old farm labourer's cottage, I felt only the faintest of echoes from the past. But here, at least, was a hearth – or the gap where it had been. I thought of the many people who must have stood in front of it, warming faces and hands after working in frost-bound fields.

Families were big then – Ann Lewis's mother, Dolly Rebbeck, who lived here from the early 1930s, was one of eleven children. Ann is one of the Imber stalwarts who return year after year, and though she never lived here it is in her heart. I would have liked to talk to her in Dolly's old house, which was on the lane leading up to the church, but it was bombed to oblivion a long time ago. So we stood in the main street as she spoke of Imber in her mother's time, evoking a simpler, vanished world in which children may not have had much in terms of material possessions but their imaginations made up for it.

'My mum came to live here when she was four years old with her parents and siblings and was here for about ten years,' said Ann. 'My granddad worked on a farm here. Dolly loved it, she was very happy. It was a lovely little village. An ideal place to grow up I think. She used to collect stones and put them in little holes in the bank leading up to the church. She would say they were her "chickens".'

The village blacksmith at that time was called Albert Nash. His great-granddaughter, Jane Paget, who lives in the Wiltshire village of Bromham, is another member of the community dedicated to keeping Imber's memory alive. As Jane led me up the road towards the church, she revealed that she never knew

Albert but feels she did: 'I was told stories about him by my grandmother. When other kids of that age were being told fairy stories I got told stories about Imber. Albert was just a basic country blacksmith. He kept bees, he had a cottage garden, he grew his own vegetables, he made his own mead from the leftover honey from the bees. He loved Imber – the place, the people. And they loved him apparently.'

There is no trace left of Albert's smithy. But had Imber continued in its unassuming way, I can picture it today as a little teashop, where Jane could bring her family and pass on the stories. It's not hard to project forward and imagine the village in the twenty-first century: those thatched cottages, having been discreetly gentrified, now charming country retreats; Imber Court a boutique hotel, and the Bell Inn a 'restaurant with rooms'. But in the 1940s, as war raged across Europe, the very thing that defined Imber's character, its geographical isolation, was about to hasten its demise.

The British Army had been using the sparsely populated, open expanses of Salisbury Plain as a training area since at least the early 1870s, when Prussia's defeat of France and the founding of the German state had persuaded Britain's military leaders of the need for a modernized, trained army. But it wasn't until 1898 that they took an official stake in the area, by buying a parcel of 41,000 acres. From this time the War Office continued to acquire land and by 1939 it owned the farms surrounding Imber and most of the land occupied by the village itself.

As the Second World War progressed, everyday life for Imber's villagers became more and more precarious. From early 1942 US servicemen had been arriving in Britain in increasing numbers as the Allies prepared for their push back against Nazi Germany, and by the end of 1943 much of southern England resembled a vast holding camp for troops. Many American units were based in and around Salisbury Plain where they conducted practice manoeuvres for Operation Overlord, the Allied invasion of Nazi-occupied Europe that was to be launched on 6 June 1944: D-Day. Getting in and out of the village was a task in itself as it was accessible only twice a day. The rest of the time, live fire was going on all around, with only a 1,000-yard safety zone around the village to protect its inhabitants. Then, in the spring of 1942, an incident took place that would profoundly affect Imber's future as a viable community.

To fill in what happened, I met up with Richard Osgood, a senior archaeologist at the Ministry of Defence (MoD), on a hill overlooking the church a little way outside the village. Richard is responsible for sites of historic and cultural interest on MoD land. He unfolded a map from 1940 showing this part of Salisbury Plain. 'The area in red is owned by the War Department,' he said (almost the entire map was coloured red). 'If you look over to the west you will see the small enclave: Imber.' He swept his arm, taking in the surrounding plain, then pointed down at the church. 'It's right in the middle of the training area. And that is marked out of bounds to the military. So it was a small oasis of village life in a colossal area of high-intensity training.'

On 13 April 1942, military planners used the training area to stage an exercise designed to demonstrate the firepower of RAF fighter aircraft against enemy troops and transport columns. Dummy soldiers and lines of old lorries and tanks had been assembled on the ground and the idea was that six Spitfires and six Hurricanes would swoop down and attack the targets with live ammunition. An audience of military top brass had been invited to witness the spectacle, which was effectively a practice run for a similar exercise scheduled for a later date that Prime Minister Winston Churchill was due to attend. They were corralled in an enclosure several hundred yards from the target area. All went according to plan until the final plane appeared low in the sky. 'This was a Hurricane piloted by Flight Sergeant William McClachlan,' said Richard. 'He approaches and attacks what he thinks was the target on the ground. But it is in fact the watching crowd of dignitaries. There were twenty-five people killed, including a brigadier. Seventy-one wounded.'

It was a catastrophic error that nowadays would be referred to as a 'blue-on-blue incident'. Sadly, in the tumult of war, such tragedies were not uncommon though the scale of this one was particularly distressing. Three days later Churchill attended a similar exercise on the Imber training area that passed off without incident and in the village itself people carried on, apparently unperturbed. But Imber's card was marked. It had become apparent to the military authorities that village life was incompatible with preparations for war.

This is where John Williams enters the story. I met him back in the village, outside the brick shell near the church that is all that remains of the old schoolhouse. There was not so much as a stub of chalk on the ground to hint at its previous function and John said he had trouble finding it when he first returned in 2002 after a gap of fifty-nine years. 'I came here as a seven-year-old with my mother, Myfanwy Williams, when she was appointed schoolmistress,' he said. The year was 1943 and he remembers being struck by all the thatched roofs – where he and his mother had come from, Caernarfon in north Wales, the roofs were made from locally quarried slate.

John Williams is the only person still alive who was present at the momentous, pivotal moment when Imber's fate was sealed. The date was 1 November 1943 and he had brought along a copy of the relevant entry from his mother's school record book which he now read out: 'I dismissed the children at 10 a.m. as the school was needed for a meeting of military importance. I was informed at 12 a.m. that the school was to be closed.' What happened at this meeting in the schoolhouse, what pledges and assumptions were made, lie at the heart of the Imber story.

John said he could still picture the Army representative addressing the meeting and was adamant about the words he used: 'The officer said, "You'll have to leave the village before Christmas because it's wanted for the military – you all know there's a war on." That's why they [the villagers] went but they went on the promise they could come back. I well remember, during that meeting, the promise being made. The Army man at the front saying you could come back.'

One morning (the date is unclear) shortly after this meeting, the postman delivered an extraordinary letter from the War Office to every household in the village. Undated, and signed by 'Lt Col A. P. Thorne, Command Land Agent, Southern Command', it ordered the entire population – of more than 100 people – to evacuate their homes by 17 December, the week before Christmas. There is some confusion about this letter as it appears that only one has survived. Supposedly the others were collected by the Army shortly after they had been delivered – a story that has certainly fed the grievances of villagers and their descendants down the years.

Be that as it may, Jane Paget, the great-granddaughter of the blacksmith Albert Nash, showed me a copy of the letter which she said was sent to Albert and his family. It doesn't beat about the bush: 'I regret to have to inform you that it is necessary to evacuate a major part of the department's Imber Estate, including your dwelling. To this end I enclose formal notice to quit.' Jane said Albert was devastated: 'My great-grandmother, Martha, went to the smithy and found him slumped over his anvil, crying.'

The villagers, many of whom had never spent a night away from Imber, had just forty-seven days to find alternative accommodation and sell off their farm stock and machinery. Most found places to stay in Warminster or Devizes, or the little villages that ring that part of the plain. The church's most precious artefacts (such as the font and pulpit, and two thirteenth-century effigies) were removed for safekeeping, its windows boarded up and the graveyard protected by barbed wire. Last orders were called in the Bell Inn and Imber fell silent and empty for the first time since ancient Britons had made fire and shelter there. That first Christmas for the villagers, away from their familiar hearths and traditional services at the church, was no doubt a bleak one.

Albert took the exile particularly badly, according to Jane: 'They'd been gone less than six weeks and my great-grandmother, Martha, woke up one night to see Albert walking around the bedroom. She said, "Albert, what are you doing? Get back into bed, it's the middle of the night." He replied, "I'm going home, Martha." She said, "You *are* home, Albert, get back into bed." When she woke up in the morning he was dead in the bed beside her.' Albert's body was brought back to the village to be buried in the churchyard. Jane took me to see his grave. The inscription on his headstone reads simply: 'In memory of Imber blacksmith Albert Nash 1875–1944.'

At the end of the war Imber's erstwhile, now scattered, inhabitants awaited confirmation that they could return. After all, the Americans had gone home and peace now prevailed across a war-weary world. The notion of ever again having to stage military exercises on the scale of those that preceded D-Day seemed highly improbable. But everyone appreciated that the wheels of bureaucracy turned slowly and as the War Office procrastinated the villagers remained patient. By this time the buildings of the village had sustained damage from shells and bullets, and local vandals had ransacked the houses. Gardens were overgrown and the whole site was overrun with rabbits.

Imber was still redeemable as a place of human habitation, but as the months passed and the wind and rain took their toll, the likelihood of the village ever again ringing with life and laughter diminished. It wasn't until April 1948 that the War Office broke its silence over Imber, by issuing a statement that villagers had been dreading but, increasingly, expecting. 'Although itself not used for any form of training,' said the statement, 'the village has suffered from neglect, accidental damage and weather [sic], and to reinstate it would be very costly.' The statement added, for good measure: 'There is no question of a pledge having been given to the inhabitants that they would go back.'

This was not the opinion of the villagers then nor of their descendants now. They believed, and continue to believe with a quiet passion, that they were lied to, deceived, fobbed off. And therein lies the deep, unhealable wound at the heart of the Imber story. Jane said she does not feel bitter about the enforced evacuation. 'There was a war on,' she told me. 'The village was needed and people were being displaced all over Europe at the time.' But she feels the villagers were deceived over the terms on which they moved out.

'What I feel resentment about is that they were led to believe they could come back. I think that was a sweetener that was given to them so that they went easily. People were being displaced across Europe – that was happening because of the enemy. This was done by their own government. And that was what hurt a lot of people and still rankles, to be truthful.' Her interpretation of events was backed up by a soldier, Richard Madigan, who had supervised the evacuation of the village in 1943 and supported the villagers' attempts to return in the post-war years. I shall examine those campaigns later in the chapter.

Shortly after the War Office issued its 1948 statement confirming Imber's fate, Pathé News produced a poignant newsreel entitled 'Imber stays Khaki'. The commentary, in typically patrician tones, declares that 'Now final sentence of death on Imber has been passed. The Norman church will never again see its parishioners, for the pre-Domesday village is to remain a permanent battle school, says the War Office.' The flickering black-and-white film reveals the sorry state of the village – broken windows, overgrown gardens, shattered roofs, abandoned equipment.

Nowadays, from what I could tell, much of the original village (apart from the church) has been shot to pieces. Many of the old cottages have gone and new houses, or rather those Lego-like structures, have been added to aid its function as a practice ground for urban warfare. The site was littered with military debris. It wasn't easy to imagine oneself back among the thatched cottages, the sheltering elms and the rhythmic hammering of the blacksmith.

Nevertheless I wandered along the high street to Imber Court, once the 'posh house' at the west end of the village that was owned and occupied by generations of the Dean family. Now, like the rest of the original buildings, it was a scarred husk that could only hint at its former grandeur and the lifestyle it sustained. But it was here that the Imber story finally hit home for me.

Old photographs show a handsome, three-storey, ivy-clad manor house. The third storey has since been shot off and the building capped with an ugly metal roof. The windows, the 'eyes' of a living house, are permanently shuttered. Entering the once-grand hallway, I imagined the shooting parties, the social gatherings of Wiltshire's great and good, and the confident young swells who came here in the nineteenth century when it was an 'Academy for Young Gentlemen'.

The utilitarian steel stairway to the first floor stands where a fine old oak staircase once wound upwards. In what must have been the drawing room the pocked wall was once hung with a large mirror – still there when the US servicemen left at the end of the war, apparently. Both staircase and mirror were destroyed by machine-gun fire. I suddenly felt a sense of outrage welling up. But this reaction, of course, was as nothing compared to the anger of villagers and their families when they were finally allowed to return on designated visiting days.

For the fight to return to Imber did not fade with that perfunctory War Office statement of 1948. On the contrary, it fuelled the former residents' ire and determination. Middle England, let it be said, is not known for its militancy, nor for its contempt for authority. But the MoD had met its match in the people of Imber. And at the end of 1960 their resentment flared into direct action. The catalyst was an attempt by the government to make permanent the closure of roads and rights of way around the village that had been introduced as a temporary measure in wartime. Aggrieved locals organized a rally which took place on 22 January 1961 and saw a convoy of vehicles flout the law to descend on Imber and decant some 2,000 protesters.

The Army and the police maintained a deliberately low-key presence as the crowd hoisted a banner that declared 'Forever Imber', and the rally's principal organizer, Austin Underwood, made a cheekily dramatic gesture. He pinned a notice on the wall of the old Bell Inn – still standing, a little way beyond the entrance to Imber Court – which echoed the evacuation letters sent to villagers in November 1943: 'Notice to quit. We the people hereby serve notice on the War Department to vacate and deliver up to the county of Wiltshire the parish of Imber.'

A schoolteacher and Amesbury town councillor, Underwood occupies a footnote in the Imber story. He wore his political convictions on his sleeve – he was an influential figure in the Campaign for Nuclear Disarmament – but he'd also had a distinguished wartime career and he strikes me as a quiet man provoked to action by the circumstances of the day. In this way he personified the spirit of Imber and its people, and more widely of a nation that had recently resisted tyranny in a world war. His speech that day explicitly evoked the spirit of wartime when he asked, rhetorically, of the government, 'Do they think this is some Polish village they can grind under their heel?'

A decade after Underwood organized these early protests – with Imber still out of bounds save on selected days, tons more ordnance having further degraded its broken buildings and many of its final inhabitants having died – another local man took up the cudgels on its behalf. David Johnson has no family connection with Imber. He simply became fascinated by the story. And, as I discovered when I met him in the heart of the village, he is another of these mild-mannered English people who prove as hard as oak when it comes to perceived injustice.

'The more I looked into the story of Imber, the more I was convinced that things here had gone wrong, that promises were not kept,' he said. 'If I say to you, Michael, when those people were evacuated they left provisions in their kitchens so that they would be able to return …' He left the statement hanging.

In 1973, David provided evidence to a government committee set up by Lord Carrington, the then Defence Secretary, which was charged with examining the justification for retaining MoD lands. He was supported by Underwood and by Richard Madigan, the soldier who had overseen the evacuation of the village. According to David, Madigan said that 'he was told by his superior – an army major – that they were to tell the villagers they would be back in six months, or [by] the end of the war at the latest. He was emotional about the whole thing. He felt it was a breach of faith, in which he unwittingly had been involved.'

From what I have read, and the people I spoke to, there was a widespread belief among the villagers – at least at the beginning – that they would be going back to their homes and resuming their lives in Imber. This starts with the meeting in the schoolhouse on 1 November 1943 in which John Williams, the then seven-year-old son of the local schoolmistress, distinctly remembers 'the promise being made'. Thereafter, according to villagers, other statements were made, both verbally and in writing, that led them to believe Imber would be handed back. This is hearsay, of course, but David felt he had a piece of evidence for that 1973 committee which would clinch it.

This was a copy of the 'notice to quit' letter sent to residents in November 1943 by Lieutenant Colonel A. P. Thorne. Jane Paget had already shown me a copy of this letter. But it seems that for decades no others were known about, perhaps because they were indeed collected by the Army after their delivery. At any rate Johnson introduced it to the inquiry with a flourish, claiming that the following sentence was crucial to his case: '… if you are so unfortunate as not to be able to find alternative accommodation, and it is necessary to remove your furniture to store, the Department will refund the cost of removal to store and reasonable storage charges until you can find another house, *or until the Imber area is again open for occupation, whichever is the earlier* [my italics].'

The committee was unmoved. Its report concluded that the letter 'does not amount to a promise of return'. Imber was to remain closed except for specified visiting days. In 1991 Imber received its final slight when the parish name was abolished and it officially ceased to exist.

The MoD now owns 94,000 acres of Salisbury Plain, of which 30,000 acres is used for live firing and large-scale exercises such as Exercise Phantom Bugle, which I witnessed on my visit in 1996. Over and over again little Imber has borne the brunt of extreme firepower in the course of highly realistic battle scenarios. During the Troubles in Northern Ireland it stood in for the Republican strongholds of West Belfast and Derry's Bogside. During the Cold War it was a German village on the Rhine, at risk of being overrun by Soviet tanks. And, perhaps most bizarrely of all, it has doubled as a village in Helmand Province, Afghanistan.

Through the MoD I managed to track down a soldier who had experienced Imber as a practice battle zone. Mark O'Reilly is a former officer of the Royal Irish Hussars, with whom he served in the First Gulf War. He trained as a tank commander at Imber in the late 1980s, on exercises specifically tailored for Cold War eventualities. When he joined me in 'Legoland' he admitted that he would spare a brief thought for Imber's former inhabitants as he rumbled up that 'straggling street' in his 70-ton Challenger tank. 'For a moment, during an exercise, we would think of the people who lived here and imagine what it would be like to be in *that* house or walking down *that* street before we were there,' he said.

Between 2006 and 2014, British forces were deployed in the Taliban stronghold of Helmand Province, often on extremely dangerous counter-insurgency missions. Back in Imber, the former Imber Court served as a Taliban compound in pre-deployment training exercises. According to Mark – who now runs a company that helps to recreate war zones for training purposes – he brought in Afghanis living in Britain to double as street vendors within the walls of Imber Court. This strikes me as taking war games to an unnecessary level of authenticity, but I can see that as the Army moves from one potential conflict zone to the next, Imber is always one step ahead.

There is something surreal about a sleepy village mentioned in the Domesday Book standing in for the some of the world's most dangerous trouble spots. And my research on Imber took a no less surreal turn when I came across the story of when it was 'invaded' by peace activists. I invited one of them, Beth Junor, to meet me in Imber, and it was an unlikely encounter to say the least, because thirty years ago Beth would have been – indeed, was – my sworn political enemy.

Between 1981 and 2000, she was one of the prime movers behind the Women's Peace Camp which opposed the siting of nuclear-armed American cruise missiles at RAF Greenham Common near Newbury in Berkshire. Having established a permanent camp at the entrance to the base, the Greenham women regularly broke through the perimeter fence, once gaining access to the control tower, and despite constant evictions they always returned to resume their protests, becoming a real thorn in the side of government. Beth herself was arrested many times for her part in these non-violent actions.

When I was elected to parliament in December 1984, the activities of the Greenham women were at their height. By the time I was appointed Defence Secretary in 1995 they were still encamped there, even though the last of the cruise missiles had been removed in 1991. It is fair to say that these women would not have been the first people I'd have considered inviting round for drinks. So I was a bit apprehensive about meeting Beth. I didn't want our obviously opposing views on military and defence matters to flare into open warfare, even if this place was purpose-built for it.

When we did meet, on the approach road to the village, the same thought had obviously occurred to Beth and we were both on our best behaviour. As we headed for the village she talked me through what happened. The Greenham women had first learned of Imber when a cruise-missile convoy from Greenham Common held a practice exercise there. On 14 June 1988, she and three colleagues travelled the 40 miles west from Greenham to Salisbury Plain with the intention of 'invading' Imber along the same road that we were traversing, in order to interrupt a live-firing exercise. 'We walked through the dark – this was one, two o'clock in the morning,' she explained. 'There were jeeps at the side of the road here, their headlights on. There were squaddies over here brewing a cup of tea. So we walked right through the middle of this army camp. They didn't stop us. We think that they saw us, but what sense did they make of us?'

The image was a tantalizing one, of soldiers on manoeuvres

in the dead of night rubbing their eyes in disbelief and deciding they were seeing things. At any rate the women's peaceful invasion party proceeded, as we did, towards the village, expecting at any moment to be apprehended: 'You know the feeling that someone is going to put a hand on your shoulder at any moment and tell you to stop and arrest you?' When the church tower became visible in the first light of dawn they decided to seek sanctuary in St Giles's. They made it unchallenged. 'The church door was open. We just turned the latch and in we went.'

In we stepped, too. The fixtures and fittings had been removed, but of all the buildings in Imber this was the one that still felt as if it had a beating heart. It was a calming space with faded medieval frescoes in the nave and a seventeenth-century bell-ringers' rota on one wall of the tower that resonated with Imber's deep history. Here, Beth and her three companions spent nine hours undetected while the military exercise carried on in the village around them.

Finally, wondering what they had to do to get noticed, they went out in to the churchyard and began playing music. This did the trick: 'It flushed the Army out of those buildings we passed. The four of us were arrested, taken away by the MoD police.' Job done, by the logic of Beth and her activist friends. On her return to Imber, thirty years on, how did she feel? 'It's very emotional, to see the neglect, the damage, the bullet shells all over the path to the church. It's heartbreaking.'

Beth and I were not exactly political soulmates. But all these years later, meeting in person, we each (I hope) proved to the other that neither had horns. And her audacious occupation of the church in the middle of a military operation left me in no doubt as to the sincerity of her pacifist beliefs. Indeed, she acted precisely in the spirit of Austin Underwood and his band of invaders in 1961. It was also interesting that for Beth, Imber remained a symbol of injustice, and a magnet for activism, fully forty-five years after it was forcibly evacuated.

That magnetism, borne of Imber's sad history, still exists today, exercising its pull over the descendants of the village's last inhabitants and the many people who have been moved by their fate. The church where Beth staged her protest, and where countless ancestors were married and laid to rest, is very much the focus of their attentions. For this is where families congregate at an annual service to remember all that's been lost.

One regular attender is Ann Lewis, who told me she feels umbilically connected to this abandoned place through her late mother Dolly Rebbeck. For forty-five years she brought Dolly back, the last visit being in 2004 when Dolly was ninety. 'It was a sort of pilgrimage, I suppose,' Ann told me. 'She'd show us things as we walked down the street – where the different houses were, where the farms were, where the shop was, where the allotments were. Where they used to live.' The pilgrimage was a ritual that never lost its power or necessity, however many times it was repeated.

Dolly has since died, but Ann and her family continue to visit Imber. When Ann's husband Gordon first accompanied them in the 1980s he had never heard of the place. But then he made an extraordinary discovery. He spotted the name 'Alif' on memorials in the church which set him thinking, as the same name features in his own ancestry. It turns out that Gordon is also connected to Imber – but at the opposite social pole to Ann: 'We discovered that my wife's family had been agricultural labourers and my family had been lords of the manor,' he told me as we stood in the church.

'Imber is a story of freedoms won, freedoms lost,' Gordon went on. 'We won the war, but the people of Imber lost the freedom to live in their homes.' The annual visits 'are part of keeping the village alive or at least keeping the *memory* of the village alive, keeping the ghosts of the buildings alive. It will never be a village again as it was but, if I use my mother-in-law as an example, she would bring not just her children and her in-laws but her grandchildren and even her great-grandchildren. So in many ways the village may have died, but its memory will always live, as long as there are people to pass it on.'

Had Imber been abandoned through, say, economic necessity – had it just become too tough to eke out a living there, deep on the plain and far from 'civilization' – would it continue to exert such a pull? I doubt it. The energy that drives those lasting connections may be partly born of nostalgia for a lost way of life, dictated by the seasons and rooted in the deep past. But it is mostly to do with the whiff of injustice and treachery that clings to the story – and hangs about the very buildings, shot up and broken down as they are.

For make no mistake, Imber had a mournful and disturbing feel. And the question I was left asking myself was, what would I have done if I'd had Imber's fate in my hands? It's a classic citizen-versus-state conflict, but my unhesitating answer is that I would have approved its requisition in wartime. And with regret, but a sense of wider obligation, I would not have allowed the villagers back in the post-war years. The idea of maintaining an island of civilian life amid a boiling sea of military pyrotechnics is simply unrealistic. It may be easy to say with hindsight, but I hope I'd have treated the villagers with more respect, and been straight with them from the outset about the unlikely prospect of them ever returning.

As I drove out of Imber the light was fading across Salisbury Plain. Imber had enjoyed a rare day of peace, of birdsong uninterrupted by noisy tanks and machine guns. Now we all had to leave before the witching hour passed and it became a war zone once again. I left with a surprisingly heavy heart, for Imber had worked its spell on me. There's no doubt that its unassuming inhabitants were treated shoddily and disrespectfully by the authorities. And there's no doubt either that the very concept of freedom is challenged by this story.

I cannot put it better than the poet and critic Geoffrey Grigson, who visited Imber in 1961 and wrote: 'The temptation is to dismiss Imber as a local, sentimental affair. The village may be ancient, but it belongs to the War Department, it is dead, and so what? But if you look first at Imber as part of Salisbury Plain, then at the Plain as part of England, you find Imber speaking for much more than its sagging doorways.'

In other words, the Imber question isn't just about the rights and freedoms of its displaced villagers, it is about the rights and freedoms of us all.

Orford Ness, Suffolk

The night before catching the train to Suffolk I got out the maps to do some homework. The relevant Ordnance Survey Explorer map, 'Woodbridge & Saxmundham', wasn't much help. It showed Orford Ness – the focus of the next day's investigations – as an innocuous sliver of land and shingle clinging to a bend in the North Sea coastline below Aldeburgh. The symbols of wading bird and boot print indicated that it is a nature reserve with walking trails. Nothing about the secret stuff. But I knew it was there.

Anyone who has worked within the British defence establishment – and I occupied the very highest political office as Defence Secretary – has heard stories about Orford Ness. It is purely a place of recreation now. But over many decades, away from prying eyes, highly classified military research and experimentation took place there that involved the testing of parachutes, night flying, aerial photography, bomb aiming, early work with radar and the development of Britain's nuclear deterrent. That much is certain. But there are many rumours and unanswered questions concerning the precise nature of this work and the potential danger it may have posed to the general public.

Its legacy is a series of bizarre structures built to accommodate the highly specialized procedures that went on within them – and in some cases to contain the fallout of those procedures should anything go wrong. These buildings have names straight out of science fiction: the Pagodas, Black Beacon, Cobra Mist. But there was no sign of them on the OS map. I had more luck, however, when I opened my laptop and called up satellite imagery of Orford Ness. Cameras orbiting 370 miles above the Earth do not lie. I zoomed in on the beach, clicked on a couple of blocky-looking structures near the white foam of the water's edge and a window obligingly popped up to tell me I'd found the Pagodas.

The Official Secrets Act still governs much of what took place at Orford Ness. The MoD, my old stomping ground, remains tight-lipped. This is our 'Area 51', the code name for the top-secret facility in the Nevada Desert where the United States Air Force carries out its so-called 'black projects' – highly classified military research – and whose existence is officially denied by the US government. But thanks to new technology and old hands – former operatives who are willing to talk – Orford Ness is now beginning to slow-release its secrets.

My journey the next morning took me into the heart of the hidden state. My mission was to sift rumour from fact and in the process answer this question: if you found out what is really being done in the name of national security, would you feel safer?

The gateway to Orford Ness is the village of Orford, a village richly deserving of the epithet 'quintessentially English'. It has a Norman castle, a Grade I-listed medieval church (both commended by the architectural historian Sir Nikolaus Pevsner) and a rather fine seafood restaurant, the Butley Orford Oysterage, that I used to visit when I was an undergraduate at Cambridge. I walked down to the village quay on the north bank of the river and caught a little ferry that took me past bobbing yachts to drop me on the far bank. It's a short crossing – barely two minutes – but it links worlds so disparate they seem oceans apart.

The landscape of Orford Ness can lay claim to being among the weirdest in Britain. It was not – or not just – the bleak vista of shingle, scrub and marsh that unsettled me. Seen in reality, as opposed to satellite imagery, the structures scattered across the Ness – pagodas, pavilions, bunkers, towers and concrete groundworks – had a truly surreal and sinister air. It was as if a giant had rummaged in a toy box and tipped out a jumble of apparently arbitrary concrete shapes. And here they sat, on the very edge of things, defying logic as well as the elements.

What struck me too, standing on the brink and seeing it for the first time, was the sheer size and scale of the site. The installations at Orford Ness were, and remain, visible from the everyday world beyond the north bank of the river. The personnel required to build, service and maintain the infrastructure, and conduct the experimental research that was its raison d'être, would have been plain for all to see as they came and went. Yet, to this day (and unlike, say, in the case of Bletchley Park), very little is known of what the people who worked here actually *did* or what the buildings were *for*.

Orford Ness is a spit of shingle and marsh measuring some 10 miles long by just over a mile at its widest point and occupying more than 1,900 acres. It was acquired by the War Office in 1914, immediately before the outbreak of the First World War, as a remote site ideally suited to the purpose of carrying out experimental military work. For the next sixty years this windswept expanse bore mute witness to audacious developments in weaponry and espionage until operations ceased in 1973.

The irony is that a place once associated with geopolitical conflict is now a nature reserve, owned by the National Trust since 1993. Instead of barbed wire and guard dogs it has wildlife-rich habitats that are home to brown hares, Chinese water deer, marsh harriers, and rare flora such as the yellow-horned poppy and sea aster. It is an eerily beautiful place, mysterious and peaceful. But I succumbed to the pull of the strangest and most sinister-looking of all the structures: an aircraft-hangar-sized, windowless metal box on stilts, dominating a remote site in the north of Orford Ness. On the way there I was careful to heed the signs warning of 'Unexploded ordnance' and keep to the path that winds through salt marsh and lagoons – both the Ness itself and the seabed that borders it are known to be littered with live bombs that failed to detonate in the course of decades of testing programmes.

The metal box is called Cobra Mist. It stands some 70 feet high, is built on piles that are sunk 90 feet into the marsh and occupies 40,000 square feet over two floors – a behemoth of a building that could have been a human outpost on Mars. According to local rumour it was a tracking station for Unidentified Flying Objects, perhaps because Rendlesham Forest, where UFOs were allegedly spotted in 1980, is not far away (though this theory is undermined by the fact that Cobra Mist had ceased functioning by then). One might spend hours poking around this enigmatic edifice and be none the wiser as to its former function.

The personnel who worked here stuck to their allotted tasks and were sworn to secrecy. They were careful not to ask too many questions about what was happening in other parts of the operation, and learned to rebuff any queries pertaining to their own area of expertise. So it was and still is well-nigh impossible, even by talking to people who were directly involved with the classified projects that took place here, to build a truly comprehensive picture of what had gone on. The first person I'd arranged to meet could vouch for that. Roger Darlington was a twenty-two-year-old civilian, from Chorley in Lancashire, when he started work at Cobra Mist in 1971. After gaining a degree-level qualification in electronic engineering at Bolton

Institute of Technology, he successfully applied for the post of 'signal processing technician' and was required to sign the Official Secrets Act. It was his first job.

'You had to be secretive,' he said, as he greeted me at the entrance and led me through a clanking metal door into the dark and cavernous interior of Cobra Mist. 'What you did, what you said, who you talked to. You were pressurized to be careful.' He showed me a photograph of his youthful self, with long dark hair and beard – a hirsuteness that he said singled him out as an 'oddball' among all the military crew cuts. There were three levels of security clearance at Cobra Mist – white (the lowest), red and green. Roger had red clearance, which allowed him access to high-security areas but barred him from green zones, which were confined to intelligence officers. 'Obviously when you were away from the base the natural question would be, "What do you do?" The answer that everybody was told to give was that the base was an experimental radio station. What I told everybody was that I swept up here. It was the easiest way.'

Inside, Cobra Mist is a disorientating mixture of huge open spaces and isolated rooms (100 in total, apparently, though I didn't count), of corridors, stairways and steel doors. As we penetrated its now empty corners with the beams of our torches, Roger explained that the tin-box design was a 'Faraday cage' – that is to say, its metal skin protected it from electronic surveillance. What happened here was not only top secret, it was sensitive to outside interference. He led me up a metal staircase to the first floor and ushered me through a door marked 'Conference Room' where he recalled being shown the espionage equivalent of health-education films, warning against the dangers of Soviet 'honeytraps' – or, as Roger puts it, 'basically, how Natasha could put you in a very compromising situation'.

Honeytraps were strategies involving attractive individuals whose mission was to lure the enemy into sexual behaviour that could lead to them being blackmailed for valuable intelligence information. They were commonly deployed by the Soviets during the Cold War, the name used for the ideological stand-off between East and West that existed from the end of the Second World War to the collapse of the Soviet Union in 1991. This period was characterized by the mutual threat of nuclear Armageddon. And although nuclear-weapons testing, principally by the United States and the Soviet Union, had peaked by the time Roger had started work at Cobra Mist, each side possessed many thousands of nuclear warheads, trained on each other's key installations and cities.

Those tasked with the defence of their respective realms were in a perpetual state of hyper-vigilance and the Soviets were particularly adept at exploiting their adversaries' weak spots. In the case of John Vassall, a civil servant who worked at the British Embassy in Moscow in the 1950s, it wasn't Natasha but Dimitriy (and Vasily and Pasha) who proved his undoing. Plied with drink and photographed in compromising situations with several men, he was blackmailed into spying for the KGB and over seven years, until his arrest in London in 1962, passed on thousands of classified documents, containing information on, inter alia, Royal Navy radar and torpedoes.

This case was very much in the news at the time Roger was working at Orford Ness, as Vassall was released from jail in 1972. It was a cloak-and-dagger world and this building is still redolent of such times. I noticed, for example, that the Conference Room we were standing in had curtains – which struck me as strange as there were no windows visible from the outside. '*Curtains*, yes,' said Roger, grinning. When I swept one of the curtains back there was just bare wall behind.

So what did Roger Darlington really do here? And what was the wider function of Cobra Mist? He told me that the highly classified project he was encouraged to think of as 'an experimental radio base' was in fact a new weapon in the Cold War. Cobra Mist was an Over The Horizon (OTH) radar system – that is to say a system that bounced radio waves off the ionosphere in order to 'see' over the horizon. In this way it could detect targets such as missiles at extremely long ranges, up to 2,000 miles away, in order to provide early warning of a possible attack. Conceived, financed and operated largely by the US government (with some input from the MoD and civilian technicians such as Roger), it was meant to keep tabs on missile launches in the Eastern Bloc. The Faraday cage we were standing in was not the half of it.

Roger, who was amazed to see birdwatchers on Orford Ness when he remembered the place crawling with security men with 'big dogs and big guns', took me outside, to the north-east side of the building. In front of us was marshland. Beyond that the North Sea – and many miles beyond that the heartlands of the former Soviet Union. But look closely, he said. There were still tracks on the ground, and concrete groundworks, that indicated a vast installation once stood here. 'It was like a third of a circle, a big fan,' he said. 'It was made of eighteen lines of radio antennae which were each two thousand two hundred feet long. The antennae were a hundred feet tall, up to one hundred and eighty feet tall – different heights all the way down in a logarithmic curve.'

This forest of masts, known as an 'array', was removed in the 1970s but the sheer physical presence of such a colossal complex, occupying 130 acres, raised questions among puzzled locals – which Roger was careful to deflect when he drank in the pubs of Orford village. It was the potential data provided by this array – the most powerful radar of its kind at that time, according to the Pentagon – that the Americans and British were so keen to acquire and analyse. And this was what Roger was trained to do, in a 'high-security receiving station' that was, he said, 'another "Faraday Cage" within the building itself'.

We returned to the building and he took me to another room on the first floor which he said was the operations centre. Fibre-optic cables were laid with the capacity to feed in vast amounts of data which would be displayed on screens. The room has a glassed-off partition along one side where, said Roger, 'all the colonels could sit up and watch what was happening. At the back of the room was a huge map of the arc of the antennae showing all the strategic points. The central aiming point was mid-Russia.'

Inevitably, given the level of activity around Orford Ness and the intriguing nature of the structures taking shape, the media began to show undue interest in this 'experimental radio station'. In May 1971 the *Daily Express* ran a piece by the investigative reporter Chapman Pincher headlined 'CIA in Britain row', in which he wrote that 'left-wing Labour MPs feared "the base may now give the Russians another possible target in Britain"'. This was a hugely controversial subject at the time as the UK was a prominent member of the North Atlantic Treaty Organization (NATO), the alliance of Western nations in ideological and military opposition to the Eastern Bloc, and had US nuclear weapons based on its soil as well as an independent nuclear capability, all of which put it directly in the firing line should the Cold War escalate into military conflict. In the early 1970s the UK government drew up a top-secret list of more than 100 sites that it believed would be vulnerable to attack. On the list were air and naval bases, radar installations – and (proving those 'left-wing labour MPs' right) Cobra Mist on Orford Ness.

But the Cobra Mist project was not going to plan. There was talk of it being too susceptible to what Roger referred to as 'noise problems' – radio interference, or deliberate jamming. This was a common Soviet tactic in the Cold War era and Roger was only half-joking when he referred to rumoured sightings in the seas off Suffolk of 'Russian trawlers that didn't fish and had a lot of antennae on them'. A joint American–British team of experts was convened to get to the bottom of the 'noise problems' but failed to do so. Then, one Friday, Roger was told not to come in to work the following Monday. 'It was very, very abrupt,' he said. 'All of a sudden your job's gone.'

Cobra Mist officially closed down in the summer of 1973. The hardware was dismantled, the personnel redeployed or, like Roger, simply laid off. A huge amount of investment – estimated at \$1 billion in today's money – and effort had been expended. For what? Was Cobra Mist a billion-dollar mistake? A Suffolk white elephant? No definitive explanation has ever been forthcoming for the scrapping of this supposedly cutting-edge surveillance installation.

Perhaps Cobra Mist was deemed uneconomic. It was also, you could argue, as much a part of the arms race as the missiles and bombs, and as such would have been in breach of the Strategic Arms Limitation Talks (SALT) nuclear non-proliferation treaties of the early 1970s – which may have made the authorities increasingly nervous about proceeding to full operational capacity. In the end, the project code-named Cobra Mist concluded as mysteriously as it had begun – without tracking a single Soviet missile, or indeed becoming a target of Soviet firepower.

Cobra Mist was the final chapter in Orford Ness's history as a site of highly classified military experimentation. As I walked back into the middle of Orford Ness I was looking out for buildings associated with the very dawn of radar technology. I had in my bag a painstakingly researched document entitled *Atomic Weapons Research Establishment – Archaeological Survey and Investigation.* Produced by experts at English Heritage, a body responsible for Britain's historic buildings and sites, who mapped and examined practically every inch of Orford Ness, it proved an invaluable crib sheet to the site on the day I visited.

Though the report refers principally to the tenure of the Atomic Weapons Research Establishment (AWRE) here after the Second World War – a period I shall come to presently – it also covers activities that took place from the time the War Office acquired it at the beginning of the First World War. I was looking for the 'Street', a line of buildings connected with the airfield built by the Royal Flying Corps, the forerunner of the Royal Air Force, in 1914. There are just two buildings left intact now, single-storey huts at the south-west end of the 'Street', whose nondescript appearance belied what went on within. For, on 13 May 1935, the huts were taken over by a select group of scientists who became known as 'the Islanders'. And what they proceeded to achieve here changed the parameters of modern warfare and almost certainly saved Britain's bacon in the Second World War.

If the code name Cobra Mist smacks of Cold War paranoia and Stanley Kubrick's classic 1964 film *Dr Strangelove*, the interwar project with the code name 'RDF' is straight out of the *Flash Gordon* movies of the mid-to-late 1930s. As that decade progressed the defence establishment in Britain became increasingly concerned by the scale of German militarization, and in particular the threat to the civilian population posed by aerial bombardment, should hostilities break out. Fears were further stoked by rumours that the Nazis were developing a so-called 'death ray', some sort of particle-beam weapon that could be used to bring down enemy aircraft (Ming the Merciless, Flash Gordon's sworn enemy, had just such a weapon in his considerable toolkit).

In 1934 the Air Ministry actually offered a prize of £1,000 to anyone who could develop a system of directed radio waves capable of killing a sheep at 100 yards. Unsurprisingly nothing came of this, but the fantasy that it might be possible was to set a hare running that culminated in one of the most important military–technological developments of the twentieth century. The scientist principally responsible was Dr Robert Watson-Watt, then superintendent of a department of the National Physical Laboratory near Slough.

Watson-Watt gave the death-ray idea short shrift, but he did believe in the feasibility of bouncing radio waves off enemy aircraft in order to *detect* – as opposed to *destroy* – them. After an initial trial in Northamptonshire, in which Watson-Watt and his assistant Arnold Wilkins succeeded in obtaining a signal from an overflying RAF bomber, in the spring of 1935 they moved operations to those two huts in the secretive setting of Orford Ness.

Here and at Bawdsey, a short distance down the Suffolk coast, they developed a system originally given the deliberately vague acronym RDF (for Range and Direction Finding or Radio Direction Finding) and subsequently known to the world as radar – the transmission of radio waves that reflect off targets and return signals revealing the location of those targets. By the time that Britain declared war on Germany, on 3 September 1939, a network of radar stations known as Chain Home was operational along much of the south and east coasts of Britain.

Capable of detecting enemy aircraft as they approached home airspace, Chain Home proved decisive in the Battle of Britain, which was conducted in the skies mainly over southern England by the RAF and the Luftwaffe between July and October 1940. As German bombers and their fighter escorts crossed the coast in waves, British Spitfires and Hurricanes had already been scrambled to meet them thanks to the early warnings provided by Chain Home.

Amid the wild and remote surroundings of Orford Ness I paused to reflect that the story of radar is a classic case of British muddle coming up trumps. The country may, notoriously, have underinvested in rearmament during the 1930s, but hidden away in odd, windswept corners geniuses like Watson-Watt and Wilkins were giving us the edge in less conventional ways. (Barnes Wallis, inventor of the bouncing bombs dropped in the Dambusters Raid of 1943, was in the same mould.) When Winston Churchill concluded, famously, of the Battle of Britain that 'Never in the field of human conflict was so much owed by so many to so few', he was referring to those brave fighter pilots who fought off the Nazi foe. But they couldn't have succeeded without the unsung heroes of Orford Ness and other secret establishments who had had a vision and made it a reality.

The cessation of hostilities in 1945 did not, however, signal the end of military innovation. As the 'hot' war against Nazi Germany and the Axis powers gave way to the Cold War against the Soviet Bloc, the need for individuals capable of thinking 'outside the box' was as great as ever. From the old radar huts on the Street I walked due south, crossing the watercourse known as Stony Ditch, into the nuclear age. And it did look appropriately apocalyptic. I was now on the shingle beach and it was scattered with an extraordinary collection of vast buildings that dwarf the human form. This could easily be a film set, standing in for a distant and inhospitable planet. And the work that took place here, driven by scientists of courage and ingenuity, was hardly less amazing or disturbing.

Twenty years ago, as the Defence Secretary in John Major's government, I was happy to make the argument that nuclear weapons were vital for our national security. They enabled us to retain a permanent seat on the UN Security Council and play a vital part in the NATO alliance, which was dedicated to providing collective military protection in the event of Soviet attack.

The Soviet Union had finally collapsed in 1991, at least partly due to NATO's unrelenting commitment to hard defence and maintaining military capabilities, including the nuclear option.

It was certainly not the time to relax our nuclear vigilance. But I didn't spend much time thinking about the work required to devise and maintain such apocalyptic armaments. Indeed I had only a hazy idea of where and how our nuclear capability had come about. Now I found myself standing in the very crucible of this weapon to end all weapons, the place where nuclear bombs bearing cryptic names such as Blue Danube, Red Beard and Yellow Sun were, literally, tested to destruction.

The complex of structures surrounding me were where the testing took place. They were built and used between the mid-1950s and early 1970s by the AWRE, the government body in charge of Britain's nuclear weapons programme. And after the AWRE ceased operations in 1971 they were dismantled, reduced for the most part to a jumble of concrete and steel that lies littered like the pieces of a fiendish jigsaw puzzle.

I had arranged to meet the National Trust archaeologist Angus Wainwright here on the shingle. He was a key figure for me, having spent decades trying to solve the riddle of this place. I noticed he couldn't help smiling at my expression of bafflement as I gazed around from pagodas to towers to bunkers. But he admitted that even he was left guessing by certain structures and pieces of hardware. 'Really the key to understanding [Orford Ness] is the people who worked here,' he told me. 'The trouble is, on a site like this, which is very secret, if you didn't work in a particular building you would know nothing.' He also pointed out that the buildings were decommissioned in such a way as to make it difficult to make sense of them afterwards. 'Often I can be dealing with a site that is hundreds of years old and I'll know more about it than [the much more recent archaeology] here,' he said.

He took me into 'Laboratory 3', made of reinforced concrete, semi-submerged in the shingle, with a barrel-vaulted roof. 'This one has a few clues in it because you can see the insulation everywhere,' he said. 'This is the lab where they were heating up or cooling down bombs.' Angus told me that the AWRE research conducted here had two elements: testing the ballistics of bombs (the accuracy with which they flew after being dropped), which involved the dropping of dummy bombs from aircraft over the North Sea and on Orford Ness's own bombing range; and testing the 'safety' and reliability of bombs by subjecting them to various strains and stresses – including extremes of temperature – so that when the day came for them to be dropped on Kiev or Moscow or Leningrad they would go off faultlessly. This testing was known, with typical insouciance, as 'shake, rattle and roll'.

On 3 October 1952, Britain had become the world's third nuclear power, after the USA and the USSR, when her first nuclear device was successfully tested in the Monte Bello Islands, off Western Australia. Three years later a dummy of the first operational nuclear bomb, Blue Danube, was tested at Orford Ness. Among the aeronautical engineers who worked on the Blue Danube project was Professor John Allen, now ninety-five. Professor Allen, a modest man, is one of the cleverest scientists of his generation and it was a particular privilege to meet this rare survivor of a pioneering age among the buildings where he and his team carried out their dangerous but vital work.

'I was called to a secret meeting and I was told that they wanted me to be a leader in the design and the ballistics of our atom bomb which was called Blue Danube,' he told me. He described 'a fine collaborative spirit' among the scientists, engineers and 'oddballs' involved. 'We realized we were pioneering dangerous "beasties", but although some people called them weapons of mass destruction I've always only seen them as deterrents.'

The bombs which were dropped over Orford Ness were dummies. 'But they had the right shape, the right size, all the right equipment,' explained Professor Allen. 'Orford Ness's job was to track not only the flight of the bomb itself but how it left the aircraft, and that was a terribly difficult thing to get right.' There was plenty of scope for error and on one occasion, he admitted, a bomb was dropped by mistake and landed in someone's back garden. 'Not a thing you would welcome and I'm not sure their insurance would have covered it,' he said, wryly.

Blue Danube had an explosive yield roughly equivalent to the atomic bombs dropped by the Americans on Japan at the end of the Second World War. By the chilling logic of the arms race, however, it wasn't 'enough' to have bombs that could flatten entire cities, as had happened in Nagasaki and Hiroshima. In the battle to stay ahead of our enemies we were developing a weapons system that was a thousand times more powerful: the hydrogen or H-bomb.

In 1963 an eighteen-year-old school leaver from Ipswich found himself pitched into the very heart of this project. Les Barton was my final witness and it was his task to show me the buildings that, above all others, captured my imagination on Orford Ness: the Pagodas, otherwise known as the Vibration Test Buildings. From the outside, the raised roofs gave them the appearance of ancient temples. They were similar in design so we chose just one to enter. And as he led me through the entrance passage and into the central cell we fell silent, necks craning, taking in a design of obvious purpose and austere grandeur.

Built in 1960 for the testing of weapons of fearsome power, the Pagodas are reinforced concrete chambers measuring 54 feet by 24 feet, covered by massive concrete roofs raised clear of the walls on sixteen concrete columns. Beneath our feet the floor of the one we entered was covered in parallel steel beams. The overall design, said Les, was geared to absorbing an explosion in the event of an accident. Not only are the walls immensely thick and strong but the roof stands proud of the walls for a reason: 'If a serious bang ever did occur the columns were designed to fall away and the roof of the pagoda was intended to plummet into where we are now, in the base of the building, to contain what was happening.'

So what on earth went on here? Before we got to that, Les explained how a 'callow youth' with qualifications in physics and chemistry found himself at the centre of the AWRE's research into the latest weapons technology. 'I was working in a chemistry lab, which was not particularly thrilling, when my grandfather saw an advert in the *Ipswich Star*,' he told me. He was interviewed by a government panel of 'three or four guys' and the next thing he knew 'a bloke with a bowler hat and a moustache – a James Bond caricature – showed up unannounced in Ipswich' to carry out security vetting by talking to his parents and employers. 'Obviously I passed,' he said.

Les was assigned to a team that subjected atomic and hydrogen bombs to extreme environmental pressures. 'In order to make the weapons rugged enough to get to where they were supposed to go, and not blow up in the meantime, they would undergo the most *extreme* stress – vibration, thermal shock, centrifuge,' he said. In the Pagodas they were, among other things, tested for their ability to withstand the accidental detonation of 400 pounds of high explosives.

The size and strength of the Pagoda was beginning to make sense. Les now made what to me was an extraordinary claim that on occasion the bombs being tested contained both high explosives and fissile material (i.e. elements capable of sustaining a nuclear reaction). But he discounted the possibility that a catastrophe could have occurred if any of the testing procedures had gone wrong. 'There was never any danger of a nuclear explosion because although the weapons were fully charged they were not able to be triggered. The worst that could have happened was that if the weapon had ruptured there was a possibility of leakage of radioactive material.' He seemed pretty sanguine on this point but I could feel my eyebrows shooting up and staying there. This wasn't just highly classified work, it was also mortally dangerous,

Right: From the mid-nineteenth century, when it became popular as a seaside resort, 'Merry Doctor Brighton' was considered a place of great health-giving properties. In fact, its poor sewerage led to numerous cholera outbreaks – until an extensive sewer system was built and Brighton recovered its reputation for 'health and pleasure'.

Below: Between 1869 and 1874 more than £100,000 (the equivalent of £6.5 million today) was spent to construct a vast network of sewers beneath Brighton.

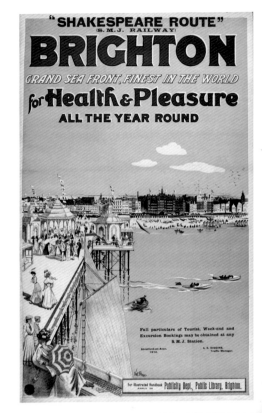

Above and left: During the war and after, Imber village suffered terribly, both from neglect and bombardment. The old cottages were shot to pieces.

Below: On 22 January 1961, aggrieved locals and former villagers descended on Imber village to stage a protest. They hoisted a banner and carried placards that declared 'Forever Imber'.

Left: An aerial view of the forest of masts, or array, of the Cobra Mist radar system. Now dismantled, this was just one of a plethora of bizarre structures on Orford Ness that are testament to the experiments and initiatives that took place there.

Left: Robert Watson-Watt, who pioneered radar technology at Orford Ness. He was instrumental in creating a network of radar stations known as Chain Home that was operational along much of the south and east coasts of Britain by the beginning of World War Two.

Right: Professor John Allen, Head of the Bomb Targeting Unit, was part of the team that carried out tests on Blue Danube.

Below: The first operational nuclear bomb, Blue Danube, was tested at Orford Ness.

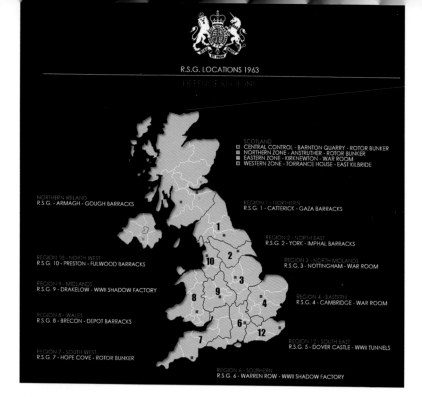

R.S.G. LOCATIONS 1963
DEFENCE REGIONS

SCOTLAND
☐ CENTRAL CONTROL - BARNTON QUARRY - ROTOR BUNKER
■ NORTHERN ZONE - ANSTRUTHER - ROTOR BUNKER
■ EASTERN ZONE - KIRKNEWTON - WAR ROOM
☐ WESTERN ZONE - TORRANCE HOUSE - EAST KILBRIDE

NORTHERN IRELAND
R.S.G. - ARMAGH - GOUGH BARRACKS

REGION 1 - NORTHERN
R.S.G. 1 - CATTERICK - GAZA BARRACKS

REGION 2 - NORTH EAST
R.S.G. 2 - YORK - IMPHAL BARRACKS

REGION 10 - NORTH WEST
R.S.G. 10 - PRESTON - FULWOOD BARRACKS

REGION 3 - NORTH MIDLANDS
R.S.G. 3 - NOTTINGHAM - WAR ROOM

REGION 9 - MIDLANDS
R.S.G. 9 - DRAKELOW - WWII SHADOW FACTORY

REGION 4 - EASTERN
R.S.G. 4 - CAMBRIDGE - WAR ROOM

REGION 8 - WALES
R.S.G. 8 - BRECON - DEPOT BARRACKS

REGION 7 - SOUTH WEST
R.S.G. 7 - HOPE COVE - ROTOR BUNKER

REGION 12 - SOUTH EAST
R.S.G. 5 - DOVER CASTLE - WWII TUNNELS

REGION 6 - SOUTHERN
R.S.G. 6 - WARREN ROW - WWII SHADOW FACTORY

Above: A map of the RSG locations across the country. Each RSG would have had representatives of the main government departments. The idea was that if one or more RSGs were destroyed the others could take up the slack.

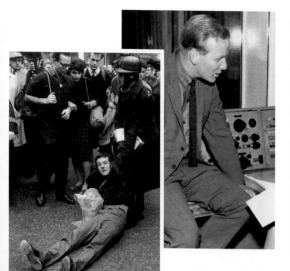

Far left: Peace protestors Ruth and Nicholas Walter. In 1963 they broke into one of the RSG bunkers with the aim of exposing Britain's secret nuclear plans.
Left: BBC journalist Michael Barton. In 1953, he was chosen to staff one of the bunkers. His role would have been to keep the populace informed by radio broadcasts.

Above: A Foxtrot-class submarine, the workhorse of the Soviet fleet. They played a central role in a key moment of the Cuban Missile Crisis. One is now moored on the River Medway in Kent.

Below: During the Cold War, Foxtrot-class subs patrolled British waters to gather intelligence on British naval strength. They had a crew of seventy-eight, could dive to a depth of 1,000 feet and were capable of remaining submerged for up to ten days.

Right: Britain's own nuclear weapons were carried on long-range Avro Vulcan bombers and had to be dropped over targets in the Soviet Union. In October 1962, nuclear-armed Vulcans came within minutes of being deployed.

Below: The log book of Peter West, who was air crew on a nuclear-armed Vulcan based at RAF Coningsby: '26-28 Oct 62. Cuban Missile Crisis. Squadron at readiness state 15'. This meant they were on 15 minutes' notice to take off.

Nº 12 (B) SQUADRON - R.A.F. CONINGSBY							
					Time carried forward :—	2316:05	
						1668:20	647:4
Date	Hour	Aircraft Type and No.	Pilot	Duty	REMARKS (including results of bombing, gunnery, exercises, etc.)	Flying Times	
						Day	Night
1962 AUGUST		VULCAN II					
8 Aug.	2130	XL 559	FLT. LT. CRAWFORD	A.E.O.	Ex. XII		5:2
31 Aug	1036	XL 385	WG. COR. LAGESEN	A.E.O.	X-CTRY, R.B.S., C-T., RAT DROP.	4.35	
13 Aug.	0740	XL 388	FLT. LT. RICHARDS	A.E.O.	SQDN. COMM.'S CHECK.	4.25	
			SUMMARY FOR:	AUGUST, 1962	AIRCRAFT TYPE : VULCAN II	9 00	5:2
		OC 'A'FLT.	UNIT:	12 (B) SQUADRON			
			DATE:	22 OCT. 1962			
			SIGNATURE:				
25 OCT.	1615	XL 388	WG. COR. LAGESEN	A.E.O.	R.B.S., X-CTRY + TYPE 28's.	40	5:0
		A.C.A.FLT.	SUMMARY FOR:	OCTOBER, 1962	AIRCRAFT TYPE : VULCAN II	9:40	5:0
			UNIT:	12 (B) SQUADRON			
			DATE:	2 Nov., 1962			
			SIGNATURE:				
*	26 - 28 OCT 62		CUBAN MISSILE		CRISIS		
	SQUADRON		AT READINESS	STATE 15			

Above: The New Victoria Cinema, Bradford, on its opening day, 22 September 1930.

Right: In 1950, the New Vic changed its name to the Gaumont and re-invented itself as the biggest indoor live music venue in the north of England, playing host to The Beatles (pictured here by Paul Berriff) among others.

Left: Backstage at the New Vic in October 1964, five-year-old Karen Grimaldi prepares to sing 'Happy Birthday' to an expectant John Lennon. But when the moment came she was tongue-tied.

Listening to the Band on the West Pier, Brighton.

MAIN & EAST COAST LINES.

Above: The West Pier in Brighton. When it opened in 1866 it was essentially an open deck for promenading, graced with six villas in an oriental style to add a touch of glamour.

Above right: Brighton railway station, which opened to London trains in 1841. The railway brought mass tourism to Brighton and on busy days the pleasure piers were thronged with thousands. In 1919 more than 2 million paid to go on the West Pier.

Below: A haunting spectacle. The sea that gives Brighton its uniquely vibrant identity has all but reclaimed its most iconic monument.

especially with a centre of civilian population (Orford village) being so close and London just 100 miles away.

Teenagers nowadays may find it hard to believe that the young Les Barton would embrace nuclear weapons so enthusiastically. After all, while he was risking his life at Orford Ness, Bob Dylan was singing anti-war songs such as 'Masters of War' and 'Blowin' in the Wind' and many of Les's peers were marching on AWRE's main site at Aldermaston in Berkshire with 'Ban the Bomb' placards. But Les comes from a family that has suffered the effects of warfare in the twentieth century as much as any. His grandfather almost died at the Battle of Gallipoli in 1915–16, his grandmother's brother went down with HMS *Hood* when it was sunk by the German battleship *Bismarck* in 1941 and his uncle returned from the Second World War both deaf and shell-shocked. These family traumas shaped his thinking and made him acutely aware that 'there were people out there that wanted to kill us if we didn't stop them'.

In particular, of course, the Soviet Union. In 1962, the year before Les started work at Orford Ness, the world came as close as it has ever been to all-out nuclear war when the Soviet leader Nikita Khrushchev and the US president John F. Kennedy faced each other down over the Cuban Missile Crisis (an event I cover in detail in subsequent chapters). 'The attitude here was that what we were doing was very important,' Les recalls. 'It was not a distasteful thing, to work on an atom bomb.'

More than half a century on, the world faces threats of a different order. The bombs and rumours have disappeared from this sliver of Suffolk. Visitors train their binoculars on migrating birds, not flying ordnance. Orford Ness seems, at first sight, a million miles from the archetypal English village with which it shares a name. But the two are inextricably linked, and not just by the ferry. Travelling back to 'normality' on that little vessel, it struck me that the people who worked at Orford Ness – and continue to staff similar facilities elsewhere – did so in order that little Orford village, and the Britain that lies beyond it, could remain free to lead the largely tranquil and civilized life we have led on these shores since the last time we suffered invasion, a thousand years ago.

A thought still bugged me, however. How close did we come to a possibly catastrophic accident at Orford Ness? A stray bomb, a radiation leak? Perhaps the answer is that we'd rather not know. We pay other people to worry about such things, and to live with the knowledge of what could go wrong. As Defence Secretary I was in such a position for two years and I admit I carry secrets that I will never divulge. But this responsibility was only temporary. The burden was lifted from my shoulders as it is lifted from all serving politicians when they leave office. The people who really feel its weight and often can't even share it with those closest to them, are the people like Roger Darlington, Professor John Allen and Les Barton who worked at the coalface with little reward or acknowledgement.

Britain's defence policy during the Cold War may have been shaped by politicians, but it was implemented and maintained by the scientists and engineers – the boffins – of places like

Orford Ness. This hinterland of shingle and marsh became a testing ground for the technology that kept us safe in the face of the most destructive military capability the world has seen. There is no memorial on Orford Ness to the men and women who worked there. They will have to make do with its strange, bleak beauty. As Professor Allen told me, 'You don't get Nobel Prizes for this, but it has to be done.'

Nuclear Bunker, Cambridge

In October 1962 I was nine years old. I did not understand the geopolitical complexities of the Cold War. But I knew what it was to be terrified by the threat of nuclear annihilation. In the second half of that month the military and political stand-off known as the Cuban Missile Crisis brought the world closer to catastrophe than at any time before or since. I shall come to the details of that event later (in both this chapter and the following, on the Foxtrot-class Soviet submarine) but for now I wish to fix in your mind the sheer scale of the fear that gripped ordinary people – my own family included. I remember vividly how my parents stayed glued to the radio and television with a growing sense of helplessness and disbelief.

What none of us was aware of then was that had the worst happened, the government of the United Kingdom had a plan. In this chapter I pass a sceptical eye over that plan – to borrow a catchphrase from a certain television comedy series, just how 'cunning' was it? My investigation took me to my old stomping ground of Cambridge. Between 1972 and 1975 I read history at Peterhouse, the oldest college of the University of Cambridge. For me the city and its world-renowned university were the epitome of learning, tradition and order. I had no idea that, less than a mile from my college, stood a building of striking ugliness that existed in case those very qualities should ever be lost to us.

It is known simply as the nuclear bunker and I became aware of it in the course of my researches into the Cold War. But what did it contain and what, precisely, was its intended function? Usefully, it is now owned by the University of Cambridge and there are plans to clean it up and use it for storage. Meanwhile I was given the key so I could explore at leisure and arrange meetings with relevant people on site. The building lies, incongruously, at the end of a road of smart new apartments, its Brutalist, box-like appearance at odds with the sleek lines of this new residential development.

There are no windows. Its skin of reinforced concrete, encrusted now with thick stems of ivy, is 5 feet thick. I climbed a short staircase to the exterior steel door and, once inside, needed a torch to light my way. A little way in was a 'blast' door with levers at each corner that were once turned to produce a hermetic seal – the bunker was evidently designed as an ark that protected those inside from contamination. Beyond that a staircase descended beneath a sign that warned: 'Take care. Deep steps'. This took me to a long corridor with rooms on either side. In one I found a fire extinguisher with a label still attached: it was installed on 17 September 1962, just a month before the Cuban Missile Crisis flared up.

A technical notice on the wall told me this was one of the 'Plant Rooms'. The headings on the notice included 'Normal ventilation' and 'Ventilation in a gas attack'. It seems the bunker's designers had taken the Boy Scouts' dictum of 'Be prepared' to some pretty extreme lengths – but would it have worked? I returned to the entrance to meet my first witness, Rod Siebert, a former Army intelligence officer in the Cold War era and expert on secret nuclear installations. He had brought along a diagram of the Cambridge bunker.

'It's a bit of a labyrinth,' he admitted. We were standing, it turned out, in the 'old armed forces headquarters', built in 1953 as the nuclear build-up between the superpowers of America and the Soviet Union was just getting underway. Britain was very much a target – not only because it was now the third member of the nuclear club, having tested its first atomic bomb the previous year, but also by virtue of having American nuclear weapons sited on its soil. The original bunker was built as a military command and control centre to function in the event of a nuclear strike on Britain.

'An awful lot of people tend to think in terms of nuclear protection being underground,' said Rod. 'But thick concrete and steel provide a very high protection factor against nuclear weapons – even more than earth.' As the threat of war and the magnitude of the weaponry escalated, the MoD decided to upgrade the facilities in the Cambridge bunker. 'We are now moving into the more modern part, the Regional Seat of Government, which was built in the early sixties for the eventuality of a nuclear war,' said Rod. The abbreviated names on the various doors gave the game away, although I had to trawl my memory of government departments to fit the right ones to the abbreviations: 'MIN. PEN. NAT. INS' was the Ministry of Pensions and National Insurance; 'MIN. OF LABOUR' and 'BRD. OF TRADE' were somewhat easier to fathom.

The Cambridge bunker was designated RSG-4 (Regional Seat of Government-4), one of twelve top-secret facilities across Britain and Northern Ireland that in theory, at least, would have ensured the continued functioning of the country during nuclear war. 'Under the Emergency Powers Act, central government would have devolved to headquarters such as this where a Commissioner would have worked to reconstruct the business of government,' Rod explained. 'The main purpose was to preserve the offices of state and the bureaucracy of central government.' Each RSG would have had representatives of the main government departments. If one or more RSGs were destroyed the others could take up the slack. That was the idea.

At this point I felt I needed a break from the claustrophobic bunker atmosphere, and some time to reflect on the thinking behind the whole RSG concept. Outside, I sat on a bench next to a children's playground and discussed the febrile atmosphere of the time with the investigative reporter and Cold War expert, Jim Wilson. He, too, remembered the naked fear that stalked the land in 1962 and that fear, he insisted, was absolutely justified. 'We had American nuclear-tipped missiles on bases all the way down the east coast,' he said. 'Everybody realized these bases were vulnerable.'

The then prime minister Harold Macmillan had authorized the siting of ninety such missiles on British soil as part of the NATO defence strategy aimed at countering the Soviet nuclear threat. They were there because it brought them within striking distance of Moscow and other potential targets in the Soviet Union. For the US this was certainly a dividend of the so-called 'special relationship' (a phrase first used in the context of US–British relations by Winston Churchill). But the arrangement left Britain exposed. In 1955 the MoD commissioned a secret investigation into just how vulnerable we were.

This was known as the Report of the Strath Committee, or the Strath Report. 'It was the first real study of what thermonuclear war would do to the UK,' Jim told me. 'Within the first few hours a third of the country's population would be wiped out. Water supplies would be contaminated. Food supplies would run out. Massive numbers of people would be injured.' The Strath Report revealed that Britain had more nuclear targets per acre than any other country in the world. It concluded that we would be utterly destroyed by nuclear war. Its terrifying findings were shared only with the Cabinet and the report was not declassified until 2002.

The government's civil defence planning in the face of this overwhelming threat was based around the RSGs. It believed that following a nuclear strike it would take about two weeks for the fallout to subside to safe levels. The bureaucrats chosen to keep the show on the road would sit it out in their reinforced concrete bunkers, then start to impose order on the dazed survivors. One of the people chosen to fulfil this function was a BBC journalist called Michael Barton, who in 1953 was invited to a top-secret meeting at the Civil Defence Staff College in Sunningdale, Berkshire.

I met him back at the entrance to the bunker and we descended into its dark, labyrinthine heart. 'The first thing they said to me was, "Barton, we want you to go on a civil defence course,"' he said, as we crept along by torchlight. 'It was all very hush-hush. I ended up sitting around a huge table with brigadiers and admirals – lots of war ribbons dangling over the table. And this huge map of Britain. This is a smaller version.' We paused in a corridor while he trained his torch's beam on the piece of paper in his hand. It showed a Britain spattered with circles. 'They represent where they anticipated the Russians would drop a nuclear bomb,' he explained.

This map is a terrifying document, for the circles fall not just on the major cities and industrial centres, of which there are many, but on military bases and radar stations right across our green and pleasant land. Michael continued with his story.

'They said, "Well, Barton, we want to assign you to one of these nuclear bunkers in the Lake District [in the event of an attack]." Now just hold on. We'd just been talking about four-minute warnings. I was based in Leeds. I had a motorbike. I probably could have got there in two and a half hours.'

Such stories were shaking my faith in the whole viability of Britain's post-apocalypse planning, but it turned out that this wasn't the half of it. Michael and I pushed on till we had reached the very nerve centre of the bunker, the War Room. Here convex Perspex windows on two sides gave the military top brass a view into the operations centre where the enemy's activities would have been monitored and the situation on the ground constantly updated. Waiting to meet us was another man recruited to the cause of civil defence. Peter Lindley was an eighteen-year-old naval rating when, in September 1962, he and some colleagues were sent to RSG-12, beneath Dover Castle, to take part in a classified Cold War exercise.

'As soon as we got to Dover we started asking passers-by where the Regional Seat of Government was,' he said. 'I had no idea it was top secret. When we realized what we were getting involved in – a nuclear bunker – it was quite frightening really.' The exercise was a highly classified NATO war game code-named Fallex 62, designed to test the UK's ability to withstand a Soviet nuclear attack and land invasion. Peter was assigned to the War Room at Dover, which he said was similar to this one in the Cambridge bunker.

'On the second day,' he told us, 'the Commander came rushing in with a signal in his hand. The signal said, "Nuclear burst in the Channel". He said, "How do I know if this is true or not?" And I thought, well surely we'd know about it if there was. He said to me, "You go up top now and see if there's anything untoward going on." So I went up looking for mushroom clouds and goodness knows what ...' This tale of incompetence and cluelessness, in the context of the most serious threat ever posed in the history of human conflict, I found truly dismaying. 'I could hardly believe it,' agreed Peter. 'The disorganization was even more frightening than actually being in the bunker.'

More frightening still were the conclusions drawn from Fallex 62. Peter had brought along a copy of a now declassified document marked 'NATO Secret. A Report by the Military Committee to the North Atlantic Council on NATO Fall Exercise 1962'. It concluded that 'The exercise emphasized the profound problem of command and control'; there was 'considerable difficulty in acquiring the necessary information'; and 'serious military weaknesses' were exposed. In a nutshell, no European country could provide adequate defence from a Soviet nuclear attack.

Nevertheless, the MoD continued to recruit non-military staff and volunteers to work in the RSGs should they ever be needed. My next witness, Mark Sansom, turned up with some intriguing artefacts from the Cold War era: a battered cardboard box marked 'Biscuits. Do not drop' and dated '28/5/63', and a green anti-contamination suit. Mark was a civil servant with the

Ministry of Agriculture who helped to maintain the site well into the 1990s. 'Up until the end of the Cold War, our main role was to deal with food distribution, post-nuclear strike,' he said. 'We stored items such as these biscuits, which would be handed out to the population after the bomb had gone off.'

He opened the box and lifted from it a tin with a circular lid, still sealed. 'We'll flip it open – just like a tin of paint,' he said, 'and underneath this bit of paper here we have nineteen-sixty-three baked biscuits.' He took a bite: 'Still good.' Rather more tentatively, so did I. They were quite dry, but tasty. But how were the biscuits supposed to reach the survivors on the outside? This was where the green suit came in. Mark invited me to put it on. The trousers and jacket felt far too flimsy to afford any kind of protection against radiation. They were accessorized with white gloves with black rubber gauntlets over the top and a gas mask. Thus attired, I was supposed to be ready to venture forth into the wasteland dispensing biscuits to the crawling wretches who remained after the balloon had gone up.

'Absurd' hardly does it justice. Getting into the mood, the ex-BBC man Michael Barton reminded us that his function was no less preposterous. He was supposed to keep the populace informed – if, that is, he had made it to the Lake District bunker in time. 'There being no other way, no newspapers, no other communications, just radio, one of these very military chaps said to me, "Now Barton, don't forget, you've got to keep the morale of the troops high, so I've chosen some records for you to play."' The one that has stuck in Barton's mind is a sentimental wartime ballad called 'I'll Walk Beside You' by the Irish tenor John McCormack. 'I don't know about you but I get a sense of the macabre when I hear those words,' said Michael. He was referring particularly to the line 'I'll walk beside you through the golden land ...'.

It turns out that in October 1962, as the world teetered on the brink of nuclear annihilation, Whitehall mandarins were proposing to console us with dry biscuits and sombre music. In this chapter I have already evoked the spirit of the television comedy series *Blackadder*. By this stage in my investigation of RSG-4 I was beginning to feel that Baldrick must have been the mastermind behind nuclear facilities such as this. The Cuban Missile Crisis was no joke, of course. The Soviets' decision to deploy nuclear missiles in Cuba – just 90 miles from Florida – and the Americans' determination to stop them set the two superpowers on a collision course that for several days looked unavoidable.

At one point nuclear-armed B-52 bombers were scrambled to within striking distance of the Soviet Union. But the most dangerous moments occurred on 27 October, when an American U-2 spy plane was shot down over Cuba (the pilot, Rudolf Anderson, was killed) and the US Navy dropped 'practice' depth charges on a Soviet submarine, unaware it was nuclear-armed (for dramatic eyewitness accounts of this episode, see the next chapter). Either incident could have led to all-out war. But it didn't. As Britain – and the world – held its breath, the US president John F. Kennedy and the Soviet leader Nikita

Khrushchev found a way of stepping back from the brink without losing face: the Soviets would remove their nuclear missiles from Cuba if the Americans removed theirs from Turkey.

Britain's Regional Seats of Government, including the bunker in Cambridge, had been on high alert for these two desperate weeks. The following year the US, the Soviet Union and the UK were signatories to a treaty banning nuclear weapons tests – a milestone that signalled the de-escalation of nuclear sabre-rattling between the superpowers. The Cambridge bunker and the other RSGs were never operational. Michael Barton did not have to jump on his motorbike and make a mad dash for the Lake District with a set of ludicrous tunes in his panniers. The biscuit tins remained sealed. We were not to know it then, but never again – so far, at least – would the world come so close to destroying itself.

But for some the enormity of the continuing nuclear threat was a moral abomination. My final visitor to the bunker was the writer Natasha Walter, whose parents, Ruth and Nicolas, were active in the peace movement. As I gave her a guided tour of RSG-4, she told me that at the time of the Cuban Missile Crisis her mother and father had formed a group named Spies for Peace with the aim of exposing Britain's secret nuclear plans. 'They were prepared to risk a lot for what they believed,' she told me. This included the treasonable offence of disseminating official secrets.

'My parents, back in 1963, managed to break into a bunker like this [it was RSG-6, near Reading],' she explained. 'There were four of them and they divided up, each with a different task. One had a camera and was taking photographs. One of them was copying documents, one was drawing a map of the area.' Their most prized find was the list of names of those who would be allowed into the bunker in the event of nuclear attack. 'That's what my parents were protesting about,' explained Natasha. 'You can't make plans for a nuclear war – basically saying, we're happy for the whole population to be wiped out – and keep that a secret. The people have to know what's being done in their name.'

She showed me a copy of the pamphlet produced by Spies for Peace, entitled *Danger! Official Secret RSG-6*, following this raid. Four thousand copies were reproduced and sent to newspapers, politicians and notable public figures. 'When the document was published, the *Daily Express* called for capital punishment for Spies for Peace,' said Natasha. 'Let's not forget, that was the culture war of the sixties. The Establishment against the youth. I admire my parents' courage. They didn't do it to aid the Soviet Union. They did it because they believed in liberty and justice for people in the UK.'

I respect the evident sincerity of Natasha's parents, but I am not on the same side of the argument. Nuclear weapons couldn't be uninvented and I believe we needed them to defend ourselves against a Soviet Union that had already colonized half of Europe. Nevertheless, the Cuban Missile Crisis revealed some painful truths. Britain was no longer powerful enough to shape world events or defend her people from a hostile superpower.

The delivery system for our nuclear weapons was rudimentary, our defences woefully inadequate and much of our contingency planning for nuclear attack firmly in the realms of fantasy – as I had discovered on my illuminating return to Cambridge.

Soviet Foxtrot-class Submarine, Medway

The Cold War between NATO countries and the Soviet Union was fought by means of cat-and-mouse games, as potentially deadly as they were deeply hidden. One of these Cold War arenas was the ocean depths, from the North Atlantic to the Caribbean Sea, where submarines armed to the teeth with lethal weaponry and surveillance technology tried to out-think and out manoeuvre each other.

The workhorse of the Soviet submarine fleet was the Foxtrot-class submarine. This 300-foot-long cylinder of malevolent intent played a central role in perhaps the key moment of the Cuban Missile Crisis, when the world came within a whisker of nuclear Armageddon. Foxtrot-class subs also patrolled British waters, coming closer to our shores than the public could ever have imagined. Ironically, one of these vessels has made its permanent home here, on the River Medway in Kent.

On a suitably murky day I went aboard and, with the help of a vice admiral of the Royal Navy and two former Soviet naval officers, relived some of the most perilous moments in our nation's history. (On a separate visit to an airfield in the Midlands, I also talked to a former crew member of an RAF nuclear bomber who was on standby to attack the Soviet Union. I have threaded his account into the narrative to complete a most chilling picture.)

The submarine is moored on a loop of the Medway at Strood, with the Norman-era Rochester Castle looming on the east bank of the river beyond the road-and-railway bridge. The castle was built to protect against foreign invasion in an age of rudimentary wooden ships propelled by wind and oars, crewed by men armed with swords. The Foxtrot-class sub had ten torpedo tubes, could dive to a depth of nearly 1,000 feet and was capable of remaining submerged for up to ten days at a time.

The one I was about to explore had seen better days. As I approached on a river launch and it materialized through the mist, the phrase that came to mind was 'rusting hulk'. Scaffolding covered the conning tower and its vast, bulbous-nosed bulk had the air of a mortally wounded beast. But what a beast it had evidently been. Even in a state of dilapidation this old bruiser of the Cold War exuded menace and defiance.

'Foxtrot' was a NATO designation. For the Soviets it was one of the 'B' class of subs – B standing for *bolshaya*, which means 'large' in Russian. It was built in Leningrad, went into service in 1967 as part of the Soviet Baltic fleet based in Riga, and was later used as a training vessel. After being decommissioned in 1994 it was sold into private hands and had been in two previous locations in England before being moved to the Medway in 2004. The owner is now trying to raise funds for its restoration.

I had time for a quick inspection before meeting my first witness and soon discovered that a submarine would not be my natural choice of work environment. A Cold War sub was a steel cigar where space was at a premium, the lighting was kept dimmed, the temperature was often unpleasantly high and the atmosphere rank with the stench of diesel, cigarettes and sweat. Then there was the added fear of being attacked, of the cigar becoming a coffin and the seabed a grave.

I shuddered at the thought of all this as I descended steps into the bowels of the beast and inched my way by torchlight past a blizzard of dials, switches and hatches. Seventy-eight men crewed on this sub, knocking shoulders and heads as they tried to move around in the confined space. Only one, the captain, had his own cabin. The rest 'hot-bunked' – shared their beds with one or more crew, swapping when shifts changed over. Those who bunked fore or aft had the torpedo tubes for company – six in the bow and four in the stern. The end of each tube is painted with a red communist star.

Back on the narrow steel deck I met my first witness, Vice Admiral Sir Toby Frere. Now eighty years old, Sir Toby is a distinguished submariner whose principal foes, back in the early 1960s, had been Soviet submarines and warships. As a young officer he served on HMS *Astute*, an 'A' class Royal Navy submarine with a mission to hunt down Russian subs such as the Foxtrot class, which were hiding in our waters for the purpose of gathering intelligence on British naval strength.

'There's a lot of ocean but this is a very noisy boat,' Sir Toby told me. 'The Russians had not latched on to just how noisy their submarines were.' This gave the Royal Navy subs an advantage but sonar technology (the use of sound underwater to detect objects) was, he pointed out, in its infancy. 'You'd just get a bearing on him, but you didn't know how far away he might be,' he said.

There was a grudging respect between enemies. Sir Toby admitted that the Soviets' Foxtrot-class submarines were 'the equal of our "A" class submarines and we saw it as such'. The invisible, near-silent games of stealth they played along the ocean bed must have seemed less than real at times. But in October 1962 Sir Toby and his fellow submariners, along with the crews of Foxtrot-class vessels, were pitched into the heart of a crisis that was nightmarishly real.

The first the world knew of the gravity of the situation was when the American president, John F. Kennedy, addressed the nation – and the world – on live television on the evening of 22 October 1962: 'Within the past week unmistakable evidence has established the fact that a series of offensive missile sites is now in preparation on that imprisoned island [of Cuba] … To halt this offensive build-up a strict quarantine on all offensive military equipment under shipment to Cuba is being initiated ...' The Cuban Missile Crisis was approaching its most dangerous moments.

As America launched planes and ships to intercept Soviet shipments bound for Cuba, Sir Toby realized that Britain could not avoid being dragged into the conflict. 'When President Kennedy made his speech on television we thought, "This is going to be us,"' he said. Meanwhile, Soviet ships loaded with missiles and other military hardware were sailing for Cuba, escorted by Foxtrot-class submarines.

The full story of what happened in those next, crucial few days is still unknown. But one chilling fact has come to light. Unknown to the Americans and to NATO forces at the time, the Soviet subs were armed with nuclear-tipped torpedoes. And the crews were authorized to fire them should they come under attack. To help me piece together the sequence of events, I tracked down two Soviet naval men who had found themselves bang in the middle of one of the most dangerous moments in human history.

The television production company I worked with on the TV series of *Portillo's Hidden History of Britain* pulled off a bit of a stunt by connecting me via Skype to these two Cold War veterans while I was actually in the submarine on the Medway. Anatoly Andreyev, who skippered Foxtrot-class subs, was touched to see his old place of work in the background as we communicated on screen via an interpreter. 'I recognize everything!' he said.

Anatoly was in charge of one of the submarines guarding

the secret Soviet convoy carrying military equipment to Cuba. 'We were moved and loaded with a nuclear-tipped torpedo,' he told me. Retired Commander Felix Bryl was serving on one of the ships. 'We were transferring rocket launchers,' he said. Toby Frere was on the other side of the fence, on a secret intelligence mission authorized by the British government.

The prime minister, Harold Macmillan, was a veteran of two world wars and acutely aware of Britain's vulnerable position at this time. Wary of offending the Soviet Union, he was reluctant to commit British forces to the naval blockade of Cuba without a UN resolution. But in order to keep Britain's ally, America, onside he committed British ships to a surveillance operation in the North Atlantic. Sir Toby, then a young naval officer serving on HMS *Astute* based in Halifax, Nova Scotia, was part of that assignment.

'We'd just come in from patrol, then on the Monday [22 October] President Kennedy made his speech on television,' he said. 'We were sent to sea and set up a barrier patrol off Newfoundland. We had American aircraft co-operating with us. We were there to see if Russian submarines were coming down from their northern fleet past Iceland, past Newfoundland, down to Cuba.'

Meanwhile, Britain was readying itself for possible nuclear confrontation with the Soviet Union. In a phone call to President Kennedy on 26 October, Macmillan suggested immobilizing America's nuclear Thor missiles, which were then sited on British soil, as a means of easing tensions and removing Britain from the firing line. Kennedy rejected the idea. The prime minister remained wedded to a diplomatic solution but had to prepare for the worst. Britain's own nuclear deterrent, the Blue Danube bomb, was carried on long-range Avro Vulcan bombers and was intended to be dropped on targets in the Soviet Union. The RAF's Vulcan fleet was now put on high alert.

Through the second half of October 1962 the Cuban Missile Crisis proceeded through a series of overlapping, interconnected events. To fully understand the British perspective, which had a chilling logic of its own, I had to make a separate trip across England, to Wellesbourne Airfield near Stratford-upon-Avon in Warwickshire. Wellesbourne is a retirement home for one of the few remaining Avro Vulcan bombers, XM655, and therefore a good place to meet my final witness, Wing Commander Peter West. Now retired, he was aircrew on a nuclear-armed Vulcan squadron based at RAF Coningsby in Lincolnshire that came within minutes of being deployed during those tense October days.

In the following account of what happened I have knitted together the testimonies of Wing Commander West and the two Russian naval officers. Up at Wellesbourne we sat on the flight deck of the delta-winged Vulcan (still futuristic-looking, though no Vulcans are airworthy these days) as Peter set the scene. 'We reckoned – and it was all guesswork – that our chances of getting to the target were twenty per cent,' he said. 'If we *had* gone there was really very little chance of us getting back.'

His logbook from the time shows just how close they were to being deployed on what effectively would have been a suicide mission. He read out the relevant entry, written in red ink on yellowing paper: 'The twenty-sixth to the twenty-eighth of October 1962. Cuban Missile Crisis. Squadron at Readiness State one five.' This meant they were on fifteen minutes' notice to take off. 'We were that close,' said Peter.

Meanwhile, the flotilla of Russian ships carrying missiles and armaments, escorted by Foxtrot-class submarines armed with nuclear-tipped torpedoes, was approaching Cuba. The Soviets' unstoppable force was about to hit the immovable object of the American blockade. As the ships reached the arc-shaped cordon of American forces some 500 miles north of Cuba, the transport ship that Felix Bryl was on was buzzed by US fighter planes. 'Aircraft were flying over us on a battle course,' he said. 'At that moment I understood that it was deadly dangerous.'

On 27 October, submerged in his Foxtrot-class sub, Anatoly Andreyev heard explosions. 'It was impossible to tell if they were depth charges or bombs,' he told me. 'The situation was very difficult.' What Anatoly had heard were 'signalling' or 'practice' depth charges, small explosive devices dropped on submarines to persuade them to surface and identify themselves. In this case they had been aimed at the sub next to his in the flotilla, B-59. On board this submarine was the commander of the entire flotilla, Vasili Arkhipov.

Down in these steel cigars, conditions were deteriorating to a level that could barely sustain human life. The vessels had been submerged for a week with only enough air to last for a further three days without surfacing. The temperature was 'one hundred and thirty degrees Fahrenheit' according to Anatoly. Tempers were frayed and nerves shredded. So deep were the submarines that they were unable to monitor radio communications and the officers had no way of knowing what the situation was on the surface, whether war had already broken out.

They were, however, aware of their battle orders. In the event of attack, the captain was authorized to launch a nuclear torpedo provided he gained the permission of the 'political officer' (a representative of the Kremlin) on board. 'All the torpedoes were ready for firing,' confirmed Anatoly. On embattled submarine B-59 the officers began to argue about how to respond to the American aggression.

The situation regarding authorization was complicated on this particular sub due to the presence of the flotilla commander, Vasili Arkhipov. The captain, Valentin Savitsky, was in favour of launching a nuclear-tipped torpedo but needed the sanction not just of the political officer but of Arkhipov as well. As the clock ticked in that fetid tube suspended in the ocean depths, the three of them were debating not just their immediate response but the future of the world.

At RAF Coningsby, Peter received a knock on the door of his married quarters. It was an RAF policeman: '"Sir, you're wanted at the operations block immediately." So I quickly hugged my wife and said to her, "If this is what I *think* it is, throw a few things in a bag, get the kids into the car and drive off to your brother in Skye. I think you'll be safe there."' His voice cracked with emotion as he recalled this bittersweet moment.

In the end Arkhipov's voice of reason prevailed. He refused to sanction a nuclear-tipped torpedo strike and Captain Savitsky pulled back from the brink. Submarine B-59 surfaced and revealed itself. Behind the scenes President Kennedy and Soviet leader Nikita Khrushchev worked to solve the crisis by diplomatic means: the Soviets would remove their nuclear missiles from Cuba if the Americans decommissioned some of theirs in Europe. Peter West did not have to fly to almost certain death over the Soviet Union. And Britain had avoided an unimaginable fate as a Soviet target in a nuclear war. For if, by some miracle, Peter had returned from his mission, what would he have returned *to*? 'We knew that if it did happen there'd be very little left of the UK,' he told me.

On the River Medway I took one last look round the old Soviet sub. This particular one was not deployed to the Caribbean during the Cuban Missile Crisis. But identical vessels were and on board one of them, B-59, in conditions of unbearable hardship and stress, arguments were put and decisions made that altered the course of human history.

Thirty years later the Cold War appeared to have a winner. So confident was the Western world of its military and moral superiority that when the Soviet Union collapsed, one distinguished American commentator even went so far as to pronounce the 'end' of history. In his book *The End of History and the Last Man,* first published in 1992, Francis Fukuyama argued that with the demise of Soviet communism the world order had been settled once and for all. Liberal democracy was the form of government to which all nations now aspired.

But history has a way of confounding us. Since then democracy has been in decline. Some emerging nations reject it as unsuitable for them and Britain's relations with Russia have entered another winter. Today the future of the world is as murky as the light on the River Medway as I disembarked the Foxtrot-class sub. The outlines of new conflicts are being drawn – much of them still deeply hidden.

PART IV

People's Pleasure Domes

I was working on this section of the book during the 2018 World Cup in Russia. I am no great fan of football but even I got caught up in the euphoric national mood (across England at least) as England progressed to the semi-finals. More than 26 million people – 40 per cent of the population – watched England's defeat by Croatia on their living-room televisions; millions more watched in public venues such as pubs and parks. These impressive viewing figures set me thinking. Despite our apparent addiction to 'consuming' our entertainment privately, on small screens, at a time of our choosing, there is still an appetite for watching and doing things simultaneously and en masse, as we once did.

These chapters take us from the mid-nineteenth century, when mass tourism was taking off, to the era of multiplex cinemas; from brass bands to The Beatles live on stage. In this period the huge economic and social changes in society were reflected in the way that mass entertainment evolved and diversified. But whether you were a seaside promenader or a cinema-goer the activity was a communal one. We took our pleasures together, at the same time, and that undoubtedly helped to forge a sense of common identity that feels much more nebulous in the age of the iPad.

The other striking feature of this era of mass entertainment was the splendour of the surroundings. The pier, the seafront hotel, the theatre, the cinema – they were deliberately designed to evoke fantasy and escapism with architectural motifs from the Far East, ancient Egypt or classical Rome. The New Victoria Cinema in Bradford – industrial, no-nonsense Bradford – is a Moorish castle on the outside, a Renaissance palace within. Brighton's West Pier was embellished with Oriental-style pavilions. The idea was that people taking a well-earned break from often drab working lives deserved to be distracted and transported, not just by the entertainment itself but by the venue that hosted it.

Exploring such places was an exercise in nostalgia for me and it was a particular thrill to explore the New Vic in Bradford as it brought back vivid memories of films I grew up on. My taste was pretty wide-ranging, from Bacall and Bogart (which I mention in the chapter on the cinema) to *Bambi* (his mother's death was the most painful moment in my cinema-going life) and *West Side Story*, surely one of the greatest movies ever made.

In the golden age of Hollywood 3,000 Bradfordians packed into the New Vic's sumptuous auditorium to wallow in such cinematic masterpieces. In the post-war years, when pop stars were becoming as famous as film stars, people flocked there in similar numbers to see rock 'n' roll trailblazers from America such as Buddy Holly and Gene Vincent. But I was especially touched to hear stories of when The Beatles played the New Vic in the early 1960s.

I have made no secret of my interest in opera – Wagner's *Ring Cycle* in particular – but people don't have me down as a fan of the Fab Four. My friend and fellow political pundit, the former Labour Home Secretary Alan Johnson (an ex-politician with a particularly cool hinterland as a rock musician, incidentally), has written four books named after Beatles songs. The latest is *In My Life* and when he invited me to the book launch he said in the same breath that the title would probably not ring a bell with me. It was a rash assumption. To Alan's astonishment I promptly reeled off the lyrics of that excellent song.

My – and Alan's – generation grew up with The Beatles. We mark the milestones of our development with Beatles songs. I was gratified to meet people at the New Vic who had stories about The Beatles from the early sixties. Far from puncturing any illusions I may have had, these stories confirmed the Mop Tops as a great bunch of lads who did not build barriers between themselves and their adoring fans.

That truly was another age. The cult of celebrity has transformed popular culture. People watch films and listen to music in the privacy of their bedrooms and the old pleasure palaces have had their day. But, as I describe in the following chapters, there is a heartening postscript to these stories of change and decay: the Bradford cinema is being reborn; the Brighton pier has a vertical successor. To paraphrase The Beatles, we are getting back to where we once belonged.

New Victoria Cinema, Bradford

We all remember a moment when the silver screen worked its magic on us, when a movie first dazzled us with its power to touch our emotions and transport us to other worlds. Bear with me, then, while I take you back to my teenage years, some time in the late 1960s. My schoolfriends and I had gone to Hampstead in north London to see *To Have and Have Not*, the 1944 film directed by Howard Hawks and starring Lauren Bacall and Humphrey Bogart. I can't tell you anything about the plot. All I remember is that Bogart was unbelievably cool and Bacall, who was in her first film role, radiated a heady sexuality that had us swooning from the first frame in which she appeared.

The dialogue drips with sex – that famous one-liner in which she says provocatively, 'You know how to whistle, don't you, Steve? You just put your lips together and ... blow,' still makes me hot under the collar. And the atmosphere between Bacall and Bogart absolutely sizzles. It's no surprise that they were having an affair during the shooting of the film and would subsequently marry. What amazed us was that in the 1940s, in a movie in which not an item of clothing is shed, they could pack in so much eroticism.

I was thinking of Lauren Bacall, and that moment when she first made me fall in love with her, as I stepped off the train into a rainy Bradford in West Yorkshire. Dodging puddles I navigated west, through the usual urban clutter of highways and traffic, till I spotted my goal. It occupied an entire city-centre block and was swathed in scaffolding and plastic sheeting, like a piece of furniture covered in a dust sheet. It could have been an old bus station – except for the octagonal towers still visible at either end; or a vast, Italianate church – except for its bulky shape. In fact it was a palace. A picture palace. A palace of dreams, where the likes of Lauren Bacall and a thousand other stars enraptured generations of Bradfordians just as she once put a spell on me.

This is the former New Victoria Cinema. In its heyday, an era that coincides with the golden age of Hollywood films and musicals, it was one of the biggest and grandest movie theatres in the country. Every night more than 3,000 people packed into the lavish auditorium, with its superb acoustics, giant screen and state-of-the-art clean-air system, to be entertained, distracted and consoled. Its history parallels and illuminates the wider history of public entertainment in the twentieth century and the art form – the moving picture – that would come to dominate the landscape of popular culture.

As was evident from its appearance, the New Vic, as it was once known, is now closed and has been since 2000. My host, when I arrived, was the local historian Mark Nicholson, who knows it inside out – which is just as well, as it has undergone many changes and suffered many humiliations since it first opened in 1930. In the past eighteen years it has also fallen into a pretty severe state of disrepair. 'It was a place where you would go to escape your life, whatever it was – working down the pit, working in a factory somewhere,' said Mark, as he led me into the dank foyer and his torch beam showed the rain dripping down from the shattered ceiling.

He took me up a flight of service stairs to the flat roof, where we looked down on people scurrying through Centenary Square beneath umbrellas. We escaped the rain through a hatch and I followed him down a staircase and along a series of wooden walkways within a steel superstructure. 'These are the roof girders of the New Victoria when it was first built back in 1929, 1930, and we are now beneath what was the dome of the auditorium,' he said.

He paused and flashed his torch upwards, revealing a circular section of elegant moulding in faded cream and maroon paint, decorated with gilded curlicues. 'Fortunately, we still have this central section here.' He produced a black-and-white photograph of the dome in its entirety – a magnificent centrepiece fit for a Renaissance palace and intended to be very much part of the cinema-going experience. 'It's one of the things about the original theatre, that it was designed so that no matter where you were sitting – if you were in the cheap seats of the front stalls or in the upper balcony – you would still have a magnificent view of marvellous architecture like this,' Mark explained.

Entering this leaky shell of a place was a somewhat dispiriting experience. I failed to detect any cinematic stardust still clinging to it. But here, suddenly, it was – a beautiful and poignant fragment of former glories. I was now getting a sense of the sheer scale of the original cinema, and the special experience it must have delivered to interwar audiences.

Bradford in those days was a city that epitomized the Yorkshire phrase, 'Where there's muck, there's brass' – there was even a claim, much disputed by nearby Huddersfield, that there were more Rolls-Royces per capita in Bradford than anywhere else in the country. The city had boomed in the Industrial Revolution, growing rich on its textile mills and engineering works. Bradford's municipal buildings reflected pride in its achievements – its Gothic City Hall and Wool Exchange, the Renaissance-style Alhambra Theatre with its large domed turret and, directly across the street from the Alhambra (and complementing its style), the New Victoria Cinema.

When I arrived the scaffolding and plastic sheeting prevented me from appreciating the exterior of the New Vic. But Mark had brought along photographs of its brick and white terracotta façade, the Moorish copper domes at either end, the ornamental pilasters and arches that together created such an opulent and alluring appearance. The programme for the official opening, on 22 September 1930, featured a Mickey Mouse cartoon, 'Leslie

James at the Mighty Wurlitzer Organ' and a ninety-minute talking feature entitled *Rookery Nook,* which was billed as 'One long laugh from start to finish'.

The first feature film with synchronized singing and dialogue, *The Jazz Singer* had been released only three years before, and cinemas like the New Vic were intended to catch the new wave of talking pictures. Up and down the land the old fleapits, where punters had crammed in on uncomfortable seating, were being replaced with dazzling new 'picture palaces' opened by the Gaumont and Odeon chains. And Bradford, as my glimpse of this fragment of the old dome confirmed, was one of the biggest and finest in Britain. The beautiful dome hung above an equally gorgeous auditorium, as another of Mark's old photographs showed. But he warned me that it was going to take some digging to find it today.

In 1950 the cinema changed its ownership and name to Gaumont. In 1968, with cinema audiences dwindling despite the success of blockbusters such as *2001: A Space Odyssey,* a much more drastic change took place when the Gaumont closed and the building underwent radical refurbishment to turn it into an early 'multiplex'. A new shell was built within the existing structure to accommodate two screens side by side on the level of the former circle. Down below, the old stalls became a bingo hall.

Mark and I returned the way we came, up to the roof then back down through the centre of the main building and into the space that was once the grandest of entrance halls. The octagonal towers at the north and south corners of the building were the original twin entrances. They were linked inside by a curving foyer with sofas, potted palms, ornate mirrors and a central marble fireplace. This was all gutted to make way for the bingo hall and the foyer of the multiplex was relocated up a central staircase on the first floor, which we now entered. The giveaway was an old 'Price of admission' board left on the floor from the days of pre-decimal currency (i.e. prior to 15 February 1971), which revealed that seats in the Front Stalls cost 2 shillings and those in the Front Circle were 3s 9d.

Inside one of the multiplex screens, created immediately below the original dome, we looked in vain for traces of the original grandeur – the pink damask on the walls, the old proscenium arch, built in three gilded layers with concealed lighting in between. Hidden from view there are traces of the original arch – a few light bulbs and some plasterwork – but the huge screen, measuring 50 feet wide by 30 feet high, has gone. 'When they talked about the "big screen" in those days, they meant it,' said Mark.

But the screen, of course, meant nothing without the projector that brought it to life. That beam of light that played over the heads of the audience, occasionally throwing across the screen the shadows of people who stood up in front of it, was the silver thread that spun cinematic gems. High on the back wall of the multiplex auditorium I spotted the two windows of the projection room. We accessed the suite of projection rooms by a back staircase and found them crammed with abandoned equipment, including an old Kalee projector, film canisters and rolls of old film that were now brittle and fused together. This was where cinematic alchemy took place night after night.

It may sound ridiculous, but when I first went to the cinema as a child it took me a while to realize that the images on the screen were of an exaggerated size. Big people, big faces, big eyes. Then it hit me: this wasn't reality but the *illusion* of reality, a literally larger-than-life version of the world. And the illusion started in this darkened cave at the back that no one could see into, where a kind of wizard lived who nobody saw.

I arranged to meet a couple of those wizards here. Dion Hanson is one of cinema's leading projectionists, as well as being a restorer of old projection equipment. Indeed, his first action when he walked into the 'switch room', where we talked, was to go over to the old projector, which was tipped on its side. 'Unfortunately, vandals have been in and thrown it in the corner like this,' he said. 'We'll take it back to our workshop in Halifax where we'll restore it.'

He then talked about the importance of cinema on his life: 'I started going to see films when I was about six – Roy Rogers [the 'singing cowboy' of countless films in the 1940s and 1950s] at the local cinema, things like that. It was the thing that you did, you always went to the cinema on a Tuesday night.' In a long professional career behind the projectors, he was a regular at key movie events such as the Cannes and Venice Film Festivals.

'When we were doing screenings I quite often sat with the film directors – Spielberg and people like that. My favourite experience was sitting with Barbra Streisand watching [the 1983 film] *Yentl*. Fantastic.' He said it was 'daunting', to be up close with such major movie figures in the confines of the projection suite, but he quickly realized that they were on edge too: 'You feel you're having to calm them down a little bit because they're very nervous about what their film's going to be like.'

Steven Spielberg once said, 'Every time I go to a movie, it's magic, no matter what the movie's about.' Now we talked about that 'magic', the spell cast over an audience when the lights dim and the curtains part. The process is technical – the projection of still images, each one slightly different from the last, in quick succession to create the impression of movement. The result is enchantment and glamour. 'It has life to it,' said Dion. 'If you look at a roll of film it's just a piece of plastic – until you project it. Then it becomes a moving, living thing.'

The other projectionist I meet is called Graham Bird. He was the last projectionist to work here before it closed in 2000 and his association with the New Vic is long and affectionate. 'The first time I went to the cinema it was actually in this building,' he said. 'I was five years old and I went to see *Chitty Chitty Bang Bang*. I remember queueing around the block to see *Herbie Rides Again*.'

He said he didn't immediately pay much attention to the beam of light over his head or wonder where it came from: 'That happened when I went to see *Star Wars*. The projectionist was a bit of a showman. He had put a mirrorball and a spotlight in the middle of the ceiling. And prior to the film starting the auditorium went dark and these sound effects would kick in and after a few moments he would light the mirrorball with the spotlight to create this star field in the auditorium. He created a real buzz. And instead of looking at the screen I started to look back to see where the image was coming from. I was fourteen years old and from that point on I knew that I wanted to be a projectionist.'

The feeling I was getting, from talking to Dion and Graham, was that working in films was not merely a job, whether you were behind or in front of the camera, in the projection or editing suites, or even in film distribution. It was a calling that came with a responsibility to entertain. Every square inch of the New Vic was dedicated to that aim.

I continued my explorations with Mark Nicholson. Down in the basement he pointed out grilles and fans that were all that remained of the original clean-air system, an ingenious forerunner of air conditioning. 'If you can imagine back in the 1930s, the air wouldn't have been very clean in the cinema, with lots of people smoking. It was important for a building of this size to have lots of clean air,' he said.

A brick wall rose to street level where there was a grille letting in daylight. 'Fresh air from the outside was drawn into the building,' he explained. 'This space we're standing in was full of water jets that washed the air that passed through with atomized water.' It was then blown by the fans into the auditorium to mitigate the smoke of all those Woodbines and puffing pipes.

I can see the need for such a system, and the solution was indeed innovative. But did it make any difference? I have my doubts when I consider the likely quality of the air being sucked in off the streets, blackened, as it would have been, by the city's many coal-powered textile mills – not to mention the emissions from all those gas-guzzling Rolls-Royces that Bradfordians liked to boast about. But I was getting the picture – nothing was too ambitious for the New Vic.

The other thing I had not yet fully grasped is that it was far from being just a cinema where films were shown. It was designed from the outset as a multi-purpose place of entertainment. Besides the auditorium, where live shows were put on as well as movies, there was a restaurant behind the tower on the north side and, directly above it, a ballroom. This was our next destination. We tiptoed through the north-side tower, where water damage has destroyed the walls, revealing the timber frame beneath, and climbed a staircase that opened into a large, musty space that was once full of music and movement.

This was the ballroom, which closed in 1961 and was converted into a third screen in 1988. But traces of former grandeur remain in the glass-panelled windows and ornate surrounds and, crucially, in the floor. For Mark invited me to lift one of the loose covering boards and beneath it was the original sprung wooden floor that once undulated to the foxtrot and the Lindy hop.

There was an obvious link between the cinema and the ballroom for the 1930s, 1940s and early 1950s were the heyday of the classic Hollywood musical, from *Top Hat* with Fred Astaire and Ginger Rogers to *Singin' in the Rain* with Gene Kelly. The glamorous tone of the films was unashamedly escapist in an era of war and austerity, and cinema audiences were no doubt inspired by the hoofers they saw on screen to try it for themselves in the New Vic's ballroom. A flyer from those days promises 'the finest ballroom in the UK' with 'Every Facility – Every Civility'. Daily tea dances cost 2 shillings and dinner dances were 3s 6d.

On Saturday 31 August 1940, the ballroom was at the centre of an event that could have been thought up by a wartime propagandist for the purpose of rallying the populace. Late in the evening, the Luftwaffe carried out a bombing raid on Bradford that caused extensive damage to city-centre buildings. The ballroom escaped damage, but it was full at the time as people took the chance to escape the worries of war for a few hours.

'Dancing was in progress when the first bomb dropped,' according to a local newspaper report. 'The band stopped only momentarily, and dancers were actually indulging [sic] in "jitterbugging" for some time while the raid was in progress.' It was a fine an example of the 'Keep calm and carry on' mentality.

The New Vic, and cinemas up and down the land, were certainly an escape from the horrors of war. But war was also on the bill. Among the most popular films were morale-boosters such as *In Which We Serve* and *The Way to the Stars*, which reflected ordinary people's wartime experiences. And the cinema was the place where the public learned what was happening in the war. Newsreels – compilations of topical news clips – had always been part of the cinema package. In the war they came into their own as a means of keeping people informed of vital developments. And in 1944 the Directorate of Army Welfare in the Far East came up with the brilliant idea of personalizing the news from the Indian subcontinent and Burma.

They made a series of short films featuring soldiers delivering messages to their families at home. Their loved ones were then invited to their local cinema to watch them. It was a kind of Skype for the analogue era and the results make poignant viewing now, as thin young men in lightweight khaki drill speak to the camera with awkward jauntiness: 'Hello Eric, Mum and Dad, Bert. It's Ron!'

I had arranged a special viewing of one of these films for a special guest. In February 1944, Anne Drake née Boardman was five years old and her brother Michael was four. Their father was serving with the Army in India and their mother had been invited to the New Vic to view a message from him on the big screen. We sat together on the raked flooring (the seats are long gone) of one of the multiplex auditoriums to watch a flickering image projected on the blank wall.

As the newsreel played, Anne showed me a cutting from the *Daily Mail* which summed up what had happened: 'Little Anne Boardman, aged 5½, sat in the New Victoria Cinema at Bradford yesterday and heard a suntanned man on the screen say: "Hello Anne and Michael." "Ooh. That's my daddy," she said. Her four-year-old brother Michael saw the same cheerful soldier and heard the same message, but asked his mother, "Who's that man?"'

Anne chuckled at the memory and said she was particularly close to her father. 'I remember vividly thinking, "He's mine." Because my brother was a mummy's boy so I thought, "Right, I'll have one [parent] for myself. But I wanted my dad home. I didn't want to see him at the pictures.'

Such touchingly intimate moments had to be shared with an audience of hundreds. Even as they were overwhelmed by the sight of their husband, father or son – for the first time in months or even years – family members had to keep up appearances, choke back their sobs. But if any nationality could display suitable reticence it was surely the British, for whom the expression 'stiff upper lip' was coined.

A decade later, however, youthful audiences at the New Vic were beginning to 'let it all hang out' (in the vernacular of the day) in a most un-British way that must have shocked their elders. In 1950, the year the cinema changed its name to Gaumont, it reinvented itself as the biggest indoor, live-music venue in the north of England. The checklist of stars who played there through the fifties and into the early sixties is a roll call of rock 'n' roll greats: Bill Haley and His Comets, Buddy Holly, Gene Vincent, Eddie Cochran. Then, on 2 February 1963, a largely unheralded English group took to the stage beneath the New Vic's fabulous proscenium arch.

The headliner was teenage singing sensation Helen Shapiro, who in 1961 had reached number one in the UK hit parade with 'Walkin' Back to Happiness'. One of her support acts was a group from Liverpool called The Beatles. Over ten months later, with 'I Want to Hold Your Hand' at number one in the charts, The Beatles returned to the New Vic as the most famous pop group on the planet for two sell-out Christmas performances on 21 December.

It's not quite true to say that the old stage where The Beatles performed is gone – it was reused as a floor in the bingo hall. But with rain gushing through the roof, and red-and-white traffic cones blocking off areas where the floor was too dangerous to step on, I found it hard to picture those epoch-defining nights when the Fab Four breathed a new vitality into post-war Britain. Luckily, Paul Berriff was on hand to help me.

Paul was sixteen years old and a budding photographer when The Beatles played the New Vic. He decided to go along purely to practise his photography skills. 'Though it's dark and stark in here now, I can see all the screaming girls there in the auditorium,' he told me. 'I can think back to that crowded night when it was hot and sweaty, with the dim lights and everybody screaming away.' He showed me some of the surprisingly accomplished pictures he took – one of John in the foreground, Paul behind, both in their high-collared Beatles suits; another of Paul and George at the same mic.

'I was at the side of the stage,' he recalled. 'I couldn't hear them singing at all. Afterwards I talked to Paul about it and he said he couldn't hear either.' When The Beatles returned to the New Vic on 9 October 1964 – John Lennon's twenty-fourth birthday – Paul was there again to take some delightfully informal pictures of the four of them larking around an upright piano. 'I don't like posing pictures and the piano was there so I said, "Give us a sing-song," and they just sat down and started singing.'

Not long after this, Paul told me, he boxed up all the apprentice work he had done at the New Vic and stored it in the attic. It lay there for forty-five years as Paul forged a distinguished career behind the camera as a documentary film-maker. 'Then I found this box with six hundred negatives in it,' he said. 'About one hundred were of The Beatles, plus the Rolling Stones, Jimi Hendrix, Pink Floyd, you name it.'

Paul's hoard was a time capsule from another world. For what struck me about his photographs was not just that they show how the still image made pop stars as instantly recognizable as film stars. It is that they celebrate a degree of access and intimacy between subject and photographer that is just not possible today. The modern celebrity, from entertainer to footballer, is a commodity who is surrounded by image consultants, PR people and sundry other hangers-on, all wanting a piece of their fame and wealth. The Beatles, it seems – at least in the early days – really were just a bunch of affable lads who happened to have a unique talent and chemistry, and did not think themselves above the person in the street.

This is borne out by a heart-warming story from 1964, which takes us back to when The Beatles played the New Vic on John

Lennon's birthday. For my next witness it was a memory of great significance. Karen Grimaldi was five years old when her father brought her along to the New Vic for a surprise encounter. Now she'd come back, for the first time in fifty years, to relive it. 'I have butterflies,' she said.

As we walked up the back stairs, trying to find the dressing room where it happened, Karen filled in the background: 'My father was a journalist at the time. He had a contact and when he found out The Beatles were playing here he asked if he could bring me along to meet them – which they were very happy for me to do.' Knowing it was John's birthday, her father had asked Karen to learn to sing 'Happy Birthday'. 'I had spent months practising,' she said.

We nosed around some smallish dressing rooms and found one with a window that could have been the one. 'My strongest memory of the room is the number of people that they managed to fit in,' she told me. 'It seemed to be full of reporters and photographers. The Beatles and Mary Wells [the American singer – one of the support acts] were just to the side. And my father said to John I'd been practising singing, so he stood me on the table.'

She showed me a photograph of the moment – she in a pinafore dress with bobbed hair, standing there as if on stage, The Beatles looking on expectantly. But she was overwhelmed. No sound would issue from her lips. 'My main memory is the heat and the sound of all the flashbulbs going off,' she said. 'I climbed back down off the table. But instead of going over to my dad, I actually climbed down onto John's knee.' Cue more flashbulbs. The Beatles, she said, sang 'Happy Birthday' to John on her behalf. 'A few days later we received a beautiful photograph which I've obviously cherished ever since.' She produced it proudly – it showed her five-year-old self with John and Ringo. Another group shot of the lads was signed on the back: 'To Karen. Love from The Beatles'.

All this was touching and unexpected enough. But what Karen told me next makes the memory even more significant: 'Unfortunately, four years after this my father tragically died. So this became a wonderful link to my father and something we did together that was hugely momentous. It's very precious to me.'

This was a suitably reflective note on which to wind down my exploration of the New Victoria Cinema. Its history from those innocent and uplifting days of Beatlemania is one of managed decline. The ballroom closed in 1961 and by the late 1960s the growth of television ownership was causing a marked reduction in cinema attendances. Like many cinemas up and down the country the New Vic bowed to the inevitable. In 1968 it was closed for several months while its magnificent interior was gutted and covered over to provide two (later three) screens offering multiple viewing. In this way it could appeal simultaneously to different cinema tastes and fill seats that would otherwise remain empty. But the reprieve was only temporary.

The New Vic was built for a different age and in the end it could not compete with local purpose-built multiplexes offering a choice of many screens, as well as restaurants and other entertainments. It closed for the last time on 2 July 2000. Its proud exterior began to fade. Weather and vandalism took their toll inside. But it still occupied a special place in the hearts of Bradfordians and when the owners of the New Vic announced plans to develop the site, there was widespread opposition.

'The regeneration company that owned it were saying there was nothing worth saving about it,' said local historian Mark Nicholson, who rejoined me at the end of my tour. 'All the original architecture had gone. It was just a decrepit death trap. "Forget it. Move on. We'll give you an office block instead." That's not what we want for Bradford.'

The campaign to save the New Vic garnered powerful backing from the likes of the artist David Hockney (a proud Bradfordian) and the playwright Alan Bennett (from nearby Leeds), and culminated in a day of action, on 14 July 2007, named the Hug the Odeon event. 'About a thousand people turned up,' said Mark. 'We encircled the entire perimeter of the building inching the land at the rear. It was amazing. A triumph.'

Since then a charity named Bradford Live has developed a plan to restore the New Vic to its former glory. The council backs them and the opening date is scheduled for late 2020. Its managing director and founder, Lee Craven, joined Mark and me to explain the project. But before he got on to that he pointed out that his mum and dad met here, in the ballroom, so he owes his existence to this place – it's personal.

'We're going to strip out the old cinemas and restore the original size and shape of the main auditorium from the 1930s,' he said. 'Restore the ballroom and restaurant and run it as a big live music and entertainment venue, run by a big commercial operator.' The vision is bold, romantic even, and it gave me a warm glow as we watched the raindrops falling in this dank place.

The New Vic has an air of ruined beauty. When I visited, vegetation was sprouting from the cracked walls, reminding me of some jungle-encrusted temple from an extinct civilization. The phrase *sic transit gloria mundi* came to mind – 'so passes the glory of the world'. The truth is, of course, that however splendid the New Vic – and it was one of the country's biggest and finest cinemas – its glory was only ever skin-deep.

Such picture houses offered an illusion of grandeur, for that was the nature of the movies. Scratch its decorated plasterwork and you'd have found utilitarian brick. Turn up the house lights in its heyday of the 1930s and you'd have seen cigarette burns in the velvet seating. But the power of that illusion – its capacity to transport and enthral us – was real. I, for one, will be back when the New Vic reopens.

West Pier, Brighton

Travelling the country for *Portillo's Hidden History of Britain*, exploring old buildings in search of their secrets was, of course, an absolute pleasure from start to finish. Except for one morning. Sometimes you agree to do something on the spur of the moment and realize immediately it was a mistake. But you can't pull out without coming across as a bit of a wimp. So it was when I signed up to go sea swimming with Britain's oldest swimming club. The swimming bit was fine. It was the place and the time of year that concerned me: the English Channel in the month of March.

Brighton Swimming Club was founded in 1860. The idea had been to go back to the town's origins as a seaside resort by celebrating the very thing that brought everybody there in the first place. It was the sea that fuelled Brighton's economy, defined its magnificent seafront architecture and shaped its carefree, slightly raffish air. And it was the sea that inspired the West Pier, that iconic, now vanishing structure that is the subject of this chapter. It therefore made sense that the sea would be a good starting point for me too.

When the day dawned this seemed like a rash decision. The outside air temperature was 9°C and there was a sea fret. My preferred mode of interaction with the ocean was to sit in a seafront cafe with my hands round a cup of coffee and admire it from a distance. At least the good people of the swimming club had thought to supply me with a wetsuit, even if they were wearing swimming costumes and trunks. So it was that a dozen of us changed in the club's premises, in one of the old fishermen's arches at the back of the beach, and charged down the sloping shingle for our icy constitutional.

The wetsuit, I'm happy to say, mitigated the worst of the effects, but it didn't cover my hands and feet which became painfully cold, a sensation that gradually spread to the rest of my body. And boy was it penetrating and intense. I remained close to the shore but stuck it out for a respectable few minutes, floating on my back and posing gamely for a photograph taken by a fellow swimmer on his waterproof camera. Then it was back on the shingle and a vigorous rub-down with a towel. Some swimmers, meanwhile, had made it nearly as far as the end of the Palace Pier.

As I massaged some feeling back into my extremities I was joined by one of my fellow masochists, a sprightly chap who needs a walking stick when not buoyant in water. 'I've got arthritis,' he told me. 'It's affecting my spine and neck, and cold water relieves the pain. And above all it gives me exercise.' This seawater remedy, he said, 'was handed down through the family'. The sea, you could say, is in Brighton's bones.

But you didn't have to be in it to enjoy it – which was precisely the principle on which the pleasure pier was conceived. Having showered and dressed, I walked west along the seafront with a spring in my step and a glow on my skin, resolving, St Augustine-like, to do more sea swimming in winter – but not quite yet. As I drew alongside Brighton's latest showstopping attraction, the 'i360' (more of that later), I looked out to sea, between two rows of pilings driven into the shingle beach that once supported the entrance ramp to the West Pier.

Those pilings frame a view of all that is left of the pier. Opened in 1866, it was once one of the most elegant pleasure piers in the country, extending more than 1,000 feet over the ocean and comprising many different features, including a pier-head pavilion. It closed to the public in 1975, was damaged by storm and fire over subsequent decades and has now been reduced to a strange cast-iron skeleton resembling a 3-D computer graphic, marooned offshore and prey to continuing erosion from wind and wave.

It is a haunting spectacle. Cities like Athens and Rome have been defined by their ruins. Since the West Pier fell derelict, its ghostly hulk has also been a key part of Brighton's seafront. But while the ruins of the classical age have been preserved for posterity, stabilized against further decay, the West Pier is living on borrowed time and will, sooner or later, slip beneath the waves. I was anxious not just to set eyes on it, but to get as close to it as possible while there was still something to see. That meant going by boat and the boatman who had offered to take me was a locally based marine engineer called Jon Orrell, who has been carefully monitoring the pier's gradual decay for the past two decades. There was a bit of swell running as we bobbed among the barnacle-encrusted pilings, encircled by dangerous reefs of submerged ironwork, but Jon, like an old river pilot, knew where the dangers lurked.

Had we been in this position a century ago we'd have been directly beneath the pier-head pavilion. The sound of the orchestra would have been drifting on the wind. Now it was merely the cry of seagulls we heard. 'The pier was very well built, in really thick cast-iron sections, and even today in the North Sea we use cast iron as a great durable material,' said Jon. 'The Victorians really knew how to build robustly. There will always be something here even if it's just left as it is. But I would say that in another twenty years it won't be recognizable as a pier.'

Eugenius Birch, the euphoniously named architect who designed it, along with thirteen other pleasure piers, would be horrified and saddened by the fate of his masterpiece. When it opened in 1866 it was essentially an open deck for promenading, graced with six villas in an oriental style to add a touch of glamour. But over the decades it acquired a bandstand, landing stages, a pier-head pavilion and a concert hall, setting new standards in design and amenities.

Pleasure piers are, or were, a definably British phenomenon. In their heyday in the nineteenth and early twentieth centuries at least 100 of them studded the British coastline, from Dunoon in the Highlands of Scotland to Dover in Kent, enabling visitors to take the sea air and be sustained and entertained while doing so. At the time of writing just fifty-nine are left, the rest having been removed or destroyed by vandalism or arson. With them has gone a distinctive part of the personality of the seaside resort.

By the time the West Pier opened, Brighton had been known for a century as a pleasure and health resort, especially since George, Prince of Wales and his entourage of sybarites made it their bolthole of choice in the 1780s. But it wasn't until the 1840s, when the railway came to Brighton, that the resort began to attract holidaymakers on an extensive scale. The town's piers, built to accommodate thousands of visitors at a time, symbolized that democratizing process. (Brighton has had two piers in addition to the West Pier – the Chain Pier, which opened in 1823 and was destroyed by a storm in 1896, and the Palace Pier, which opened in 1899 and is still in rude health.)

Back on dry land I returned to those pilings in the shingle to sit down and read about the West Pier in an old guidebook I had picked up in a second-hand shop in Brighton, Ward Lock & Co.'s *A Pictorial and Descriptive Guide to Brighton and Hove* from 1920. Admission then was '2d.' and a bathing ticket was '6d. (including tax)'. The guidebook gives a thumbnail sketch: 'A broad flight of steps, with side inclines for bath chairs and other wheeled vehicles, leads to the main portion of the Pier, along the middle of which runs a continuous shelter, with seats protected from wind and rain. The Pavilion at the pier-head is used almost daily for theatrical entertainments, at which leading London artistes appear ...'

My next witness, Leonard Goldman, is 102 years old, which makes him the oldest person I met in the course of researching *Portillo's Hidden History of Britain*. It also makes him one of the last living witnesses to the golden age of the British seaside and it would have been appropriate if we could have strolled together along the pier on which he spent so much time as a boy. Instead we sat on deckchairs on the beach, gazing on all that is left of it as we talked. 'I think I can call it my second home,' he said. 'I went on it as often as I possibly could. It had a fascination. As soon as you got on the pier you would get to feel a certain freedom – you weren't *in* the sea but you were *on* the sea.'

Len moved to Brighton with his family in 1920, the year that old guidebook was published. By then the Palace Pier, a little over half a mile to the east, had been open for twenty years and a rivalry had developed between them. Some said that the Palace Pier and its environs were where true Brightonians chose to take their simple pleasures. The West Pier was for the posh visitors who stayed in the grand squares of Hove, or 'Hove, *actually*' as Brightonians referred sarcastically to the more salubrious town on their doorstep. For Len there was no contest. 'The West Pier was *the* pier so far as I was concerned,' he said. He always made a beeline for the end of the pier, past the pavilion, where there was a swimming pool with diving boards.

Sometimes proficient divers put on displays. 'This Amazonian lady came there,' he said, 'shouting through a loudhailer: "Any more for the diving in the bay at the end of the pier?" She came round with a collecting box, which of course we kids ignored. She stood up there and did some dives that would not have disgraced an Olympic diver. A very high board. Somersaults. All the stuff.'

Len loved swimming off the end of the West Pier. The days of segregated bathing had ended two decades before, at the turn of the twentieth century. Beaches were no longer designated male or female and the old bathing machines – essentially, wooden cabins on wheels from which one descended into the sea – now served as stationary beach huts or had been broken up. But there was still a strict etiquette about what you could wear in the sea. Men and boys were expected to cover up just as much as women.

'You were not allowed to go bare-topped, even then,' recalled Len. 'Eventually I got *the* prized swimsuit, the Jantzen. It had great big holes at the side so you exposed as much as you possibly could legally!' But the interwar years were a period of rapid social development that was reflected in changing habits at the seaside. Less than twenty years after a young Len Goldman was obliged to keep his torso under wraps, exposed, bronzed flesh was what holidays in Brighton were all about.

To understand this evolution I travelled 5 miles east, along the coastal road, past Brighton Marina and Rottingdean, to a little piece of California tucked into the last folds of the South Downs as they slope down to the chalk sea cliffs. This is the Saltdean Lido, an outdoor swimming complex that reflected an entirely new attitude to seaside leisure when it opened in May 1938. 'In its luxurious equipment and surroundings, it is without rival in Southern England,' claimed an advertisement of the time. It is, sadly, largely derelict now but a charitable trust is committed to restoring it to its former glory and the pool itself has already reopened to the public. My guide to the site was the historian Dr Kathryn Ferry, who specializes in seaside structures and cultures, from bathing huts to bandstands.

This lido, she told me, was one of scores built in Britain and America in the 1920s and 1930s. They took their name and inspiration from the Lido in Venice, a beach resort where men, women and children bathed and soaked up the sun together in a notably relaxed atmosphere and the body beautiful was not something to cover up or be ashamed of. The Saltdean Lido was designed in the Streamline Moderne style, reminiscent of the grand ocean liners of the day.

'Architecture at the seaside is very much about giving people some glamour on their holidays,' said Kathryn, as we stood on one of the old sun decks and looked down at the pool. 'Bright, white, shiny, clean lines. Nothing you've ever really seen before, and what an amazing place to have a swim.' Constructed of reinforced concrete, the crescent-shaped building was arranged around a central rotunda with changing rooms, sun terraces and cafe, all facing south to catch the sun and embrace the swimming pool. Whether you were taking tea or working on your tan, all eyes were on the people splashing about in the water.

'Flesh is very much on show,' Kathryn went on. 'It's very interesting that buildings like this catered for more spectators than swimmers. There were these massive lidos all round the coast and the amount of seating for spectators was always greater than for the swimmers themselves because of the flesh that was now on show.' It was a remarkable shift away from the modesty of just a generation earlier and it was probably to do with exposure to the more sexually relaxed mores of Continental Europe.

'People had been going abroad for their holidays and they'd seen that, actually, nothing terrible happens when men and women bathe together,' said Kathryn. 'The big change to where we are now happens in the interwar period. It comes about because of the fashion for sunbathing, because this is the new health cure. You had sea bathing in the eighteenth century that was supposed to be the cure-all. Now it was sunshine.' But, just as the Saltdean Lido was taking off, the war intervened. The site was occupied by the National Fire Service for the duration of the war and fell into disrepair and dereliction for a number of years afterwards.

Elsewhere the popularity of the British seaside was apparently undimmed. In 1949 some 5 million holidaymakers had strolled on Britain's piers as families made their annual summer pilgrimages to Brighton, Blackpool, Scarborough and myriad other resorts. They revelled in the simple, age-old pleasures of donkey rides, ice cream, and fish and chips. But the unreliability of the British weather ensured there was usually an element of stoicism to these holidays – of rainy days spent huddling behind windbreaks or sheltering in stuffy cafes.

The advent of the cheap package holiday abroad, in the 1960s, gave people the chance to vote with their feet. Preferring to spend their hard-earned cash on guaranteed sun and warm seas, the sun worshippers who had packed the beaches of Brighton till there was not a square foot of pebbles to be seen decamped to sunny Spain. The British seaside would never be quite the same – though Brighton itself, in inimitable fashion, has managed to reinvent itself as one of the most sophisticated and progressive towns in Europe in the past thirty years.

The country's evolving holiday habits were reflected in the fate of the West Pier. In its Edwardian heyday it had been thronged with the better class of holidaymaker, the ladies in fine dresses with parasols, the men in straw boaters and blazers, all turning about in a leisurely promenade of fashion and wealth. In 1919 it recorded its highest-ever annual attendance, of more than 2 million visitors. But its exclusive status began to slip. In the post-war years it incorporated funfair attractions – visible in the 1969 film *Oh! What a Lovely War*, which was shot partly on the West Pier – and went cheerfully downmarket. By the time it closed, for safety reasons, in 1975 it had turned downright tatty.

Back on Brighton's seafront, I walked along for one last look at the relic of the West Pier. And on the way I ran into some familiar seaside characters. They were a puppeteer called Glyn Edwards and his hook-nosed partner in crime, Mr Punch. The traditional Punch and Judy show, performed with glove puppets in a red-and-white-striped canvas booth, has certainly not gone the way of the Saltdean Lido and the West Pier. I found Glyn and his puppets wowing an audience of mums and children on the beach. As I stopped to watch, Punch was having a disagreement with a policeman. 'You've been a naughty boy, I'm going to take you to jail,' said the policeman, rather unwisely. In reply Mr Punch swiped the hapless officer with his stick. 'That's the way to do it,' he declared in time-honoured fashion.

'Mr Punch is basically an Italian immigrant made good,' said Glyn, a Punch and Judy 'professor' of long standing, after the show. 'He has somehow tapped into the English love of authority being poked fun at – in a safe way – by someone else because if *they* do it they get into trouble.' Glyn told me he had seen his first Punch and Judy show 'in about 1950, 300 yards from where we are now standing, under the West Pier'. But this disrupter-in-chief has been around a lot longer than that, the first mention in this country being in Samuel Pepys's diary on 9 May 1662 when Pepys records seeing 'an Italian puppet play' in Covent Garden.

The character was known as Polichinello or Pulcinella then. Shortly afterwards the name was anglicized to Punch and when the railways first brought mass tourism to the British seaside, in the middle of the nineteenth century, Mr Punch (not to mention his shrewish wife Judy) hitched a lift down with the seaside entertainers of the day. They have been here ever since. 'Because Brighton was the premier, the largest and the best seaside resort, Punch and Judy picked up on its popularity and in turn Brighton helped embed Mr Punch as *the* seaside anti-hero,' said Glyn.

I am intrigued by the origins and character of Mr Punch, a foreigner who had the objectivity to satirize the eccentricities and puncture the vanities of life in Britain. Neither, surely, is it a coincidence that a place like Brighton should have taken to this mischievous Italian, for seaside resorts have always been receptive to influences from across the waves. In buttoned-up Victorian society, and indeed ever since, Mr Punch has acted as a safety valve for generations of strolling holidaymakers. Through him they have been able to escape the chains of daily life, if only for a few minutes, by laughing at institutions such as marriage, parenthood, the law and even politicians.

Ah, politicians. This gave me an idea and after a quick word with Glyn we put it into practice – Glyn having given one of his puppets a quick makeover with a mop of tousled blond hair. Michael Portillo Productions then announced to an expectant audience the world premiere of *The Stabbing of Boris – A Fantasy*. It had a suitably gory ending and a topical punchline: 'Stabbed in the back! Look for Michael Gove!' But the audience appeared nonplussed and Mr Punch whispered to me afterwards that I should stick to the day job.

For his part, Mr Punch will not be short of work. His brand of iconoclastic humour will never run out of targets, especially in today's febrile political and social climate. Those with a nostalgic affection for the West Pier, on the other hand, had to bow to the inevitable and accept that it was no longer what the public wanted. But there is an intriguing postscript to its sad story, and it rises 530 feet in the air from the spot where the pier entrance once stood.

This is the British Airways i360 observation tower, which opened in 2016 amid claims by its architects that it was inspired by the West Pier and represents a cutting-edge version of the pleasure-pier concept. It consists of a doughnut-shaped 'viewing pod' that climbs the central tower like a ring on a spindle to a height of 450 feet. On a really clear day you're supposed to be able to see the Isle of Wight, 50 miles away. When I rode up there with one of the i360's architects, Julia Barfield, the sea haze limited my scope, but I did manage to pick out Worthing Pier in the west, the green rectangle of Regency Square immediately inland, the line of the South Downs on the northern horizon and Beachy Head to the east.

What really drew my eye, however, was the view almost directly below of the blackened geometric skeleton of the West Pier. 'It's the reason we're here,' Julia confirmed. 'We're like a vertical pier, really. Piers in their day were all about walking on water and, if you like, we're now walking on air. They were about going out to sea and looking back at Brighton. And we're doing that in a very twenty-first-century way. This is a contemporary answer to that innovation of the late nineteenth century.'

My journey through the hidden, abandoned and vanishing buildings of Britain was coming to an end and this was a suitably elevated vantage point from which to gather some thoughts. The Brighton story, it seems to me, is a salient one that finds echoes in many of the places and events I have explored. The sea that gave Brighton its uniquely vibrant identity – at once elegant, irreverent and ever so slightly sleazy – has all but reclaimed its most iconic monument, the West Pier. But the *idea* of the pier lives on in the new attraction of the i360. If Britain can be said to have a unique genius, it lies in the fact that we have always managed to find new ways of staying the same.

Grand Hotel, Brighton

From Bradford to Brighton I have been looking at British history and culture through significant buildings and structures. I have tried to 'read' the bricks, mortar and steel as if they were historical documents or bulletins from the past. But one building in my selection is more than just a gateway into history, more than a relic of another era. The story of the Grand Hotel, on Brighton's seafront, is raw and close to home.

What happened there, more than thirty years ago, is both a testament to tragedy and a symbol of hope. For the witness I arranged to meet at the Grand Hotel, it is the place where life as she had known it ended forever; and she began, courageously, to make sense of the world anew. Her name is Jo Berry and on 12 October 1984 her father, Sir Anthony Berry, was one of five people killed in the hotel by a bomb planted by the Provisional Irish Republican Army (IRA). One commentator has called the bombing the most audacious attempt at political assassination in this country since the Gunpowder Plot. It was to have the reverse of its intended effect.

The bomb's targets were the then prime minister, Margaret Thatcher, and members of her government. The country's political leadership was gathered there, in one place, because it was party conference time. Autumn is traditionally the time of year when the UK's political parties have held their annual get-togethers. Since the war the most popular destinations have been Blackpool and Brighton. Each town has a large conference hall and ample accommodation for politicians, delegates and journalists following the end of the holiday season. And the resorts themselves welcome the additional business just as the nights are beginning to draw in.

Brighton, back then, was particularly popular. Just an hour from London on the train, it also boasted one of the country's finest seaside hotels in the Grand Hotel, a dazzling white Italianate confection on the seafront that looks like a slab of wedding cake. This is where the prime minister, her Cabinet and their spouses had booked VIP suites for the duration of the conference. I made do with cheaper accommodation round the corner. Though not yet an MP, I was working as an adviser to the Chancellor of the Exchequer, Nigel Lawson, and had a busy conference schedule.

The Grand had been casting its spell over the better-heeled sort of seaside visitor since its Victorian heyday, when it was one of the first buildings outside London to have lifts (known initially as 'vertical omnibuses') to carry guests up to each of its seven floors. The hotel opened in 1864 and was followed two years later by the West Pier, a mere parasol-twirling stroll away across the seafront road. By 1984 the pier had been closed for nine years. British society was much changed. But the hotel still had cachet.

There is something about a seaside hotel of the scale and opulence of the Grand. It has an aura that can make its guests feel carefree and glamorous. At conference time the bar on the ground floor was *the* place to be to ensure you kept close to the party's movers and shakers. On the evening of 11 October 1984 it was thronged with government ministers, party grandees and the whole food chain of a political party and its hangers-on – down to lowly advisers like me and the journalist to whom I was talking.

The journalist and I had had a difference of opinion about the government's economic policy and things had grown rather heated between us. It was the early hours of the morning by this point (conference-goers do tend to burn the candle at both ends). Fed up with the increasingly belligerent tone of the exchanges, I decided to call it a night and head back to my hotel nearby. About an hour later, at 2.54 a.m. on 12 October, the Brighton bomb was detonated by a timer device. It is not lost on me that the row I had had in the bar of the Grand, and my decision to leave the hotel as a result of it, may have saved my life.

The bomb had been hidden in room number 629 by an IRA terrorist, Patrick Magee, when he stayed there under an assumed name in mid-September. It blasted a hole in the front of the hotel, destroying at least seven bedrooms, killed five people, left several with permanent disabilities and injured more than thirty. Among the dead were Roberta Wakeham, the wife of the Parliamentary Treasury Secretary John Wakeham, and Sir Anthony Berry, the MP for Enfield Southgate in north London. The victims with life-changing injures included Margaret Tebbit, the wife of the Trade and Industry Secretary Norman Tebbit, who has had to use a wheelchair ever since.

The prime minister, who was still up and about having just finished writing her conference speech for the next day, was unhurt. She redrafted the speech and the following afternoon I was in the conference hall to hear her say these words: '[The bomb attack] was an attempt to cripple Her Majesty's democratically elected Government. That is the scale of the outrage in which we have all shared. And the fact that we are gathered here now, shocked but composed and determined, is a sign not only that this attack has failed, but that all attempts to destroy democracy by terrorism will fail.'

The firefighters who attended the bombing, and the architect who supervised the £10 million repair and refurbishment of the hotel, remarked that the Grand's sturdy Victorian construction had helped to contain the blast and limit the loss of life. When the Grand reopened on 28 August 1986, with the prime minister in attendance, it was a symbolic moment of renewal and defiance. The hotel itself now stands as a monument to the defeat of terrorism. Meanwhile, in June 1985, the IRA terrorist who planted the bomb had been arrested in Glasgow. At his trial at the Old Bailey in September 1986, Patrick Magee received eight life sentences and the judge recommended that he spend a minimum of thirty-five years in jail.

These are the bald facts. But the Brighton bombing is an event that nobody who was in any way involved with it will ever forget. As I stood in front of the hotel later on the morning of the blast, I was in a state of total shock. The centre of the building had been torn out from top to bottom. On television, we had seen Norman Tebbit, his face contorted with pain, being extricated from the wreckage. His wife Margaret would never walk again. People I counted as friends were among the dead. I hardly knew Sir Anthony Berry, but since he had been a government whip, and was often to be seen rushing around the House of Commons, he was a very familiar figure.

His constituency Conservative Association in Enfield Southgate was forced to find a candidate for the by-election that resulted. At the time I was on the party's national candidates list, and had put my name in for a number of seats. Born and raised in a nearby London suburb not unlike Enfield Southgate, I may have seemed like a good fit. In any case, I was selected and in December 1984 I took Tony Berry's seat in the Commons.

I asked his secretary, Clemency Ames, whether she would do me the honour of serving with me and she did so for the twelve-and-a-half years that I held the seat. I became friendly with Tony's widow, Sarah, who had miraculously survived the bomb despite being with him when it exploded. A year later, we planted a tree in the constituency in Tony's memory and I met their children, including their daughter Jo.

At the 1997 General Election I lost the Enfield Southgate seat, but I returned to parliament two years later as the MP for Kensington and Chelsea. That same year the Brighton Bomber, Patrick Magee, was released from jail as part of the Good Friday Agreement in Northern Ireland. He had served fourteen years. In 2000 he met, for the first time, the person with whom he would establish a most unlikely association. This was Jo Berry.

I was immensely grateful that Jo had agreed to meet me at the Grand and I admired her courage in visiting the place where her father was murdered. But what really impressed me was her air of profound stillness and dignity as she talked of pain, reconciliation and new ways of thinking and acting. 'It's always going to be a powerful thing for me to come back here because it brings back all the memories,' she admitted as we took our seats on the covered terrace with views of the seafront beyond the windows.

Jo Berry was twenty-seven at the time of the bombing. We started by talking about her reaction in its immediate aftermath. 'Just so shocked,' she said. 'I couldn't believe it. And then the pain came. And when the pain came it was very overwhelming. This was life-changing in many many ways. I knew I couldn't go back to the person I had been. I thought, "I have to bring something positive out of this."'

She had no idea how to go about it, but her instinct was to find out more about the Troubles in Northern Ireland and investigate the causes of a conflict that had driven a man to commit multiple murder in the name of 'justice'. From this starting point she realized that in order to achieve real understanding she would have to meet her father's killer. She would have to sit down with Patrick Magee in a spirit of openness. 'I wanted to build a bridge with him,' she explained. 'I wanted to see him as a human being rather than a faceless enemy. Not to change *him* but for my own healing.'

The initial meeting, in the Republic of Ireland, confounded her expectations and set her on an extraordinary course. 'I listened a lot and I reached a point where I'd seen that he was someone who cared for his community, he was a deep thinker,' she told me. 'He'd got a PhD in prison. And I remember looking into his eyes and seeing something of him that meant he wasn't just the man who killed my dad. I shared how wonderful my dad had been. And what happened to Patrick was that he reached a point where he just stopped talking and he looked at me and he said, "I don't know who I am anymore."'

Perhaps for Magee this was the moment when he began to understand the impact of what he had done, to see the atrocity from a point of view other than his own. For, as he told Jo, when he planted the bomb he had demonized the likely victims as less than human. For Jo, Magee's reaction was a breakthrough that she hadn't expected: 'So I said, "Thank you, I'm going to go now," and he said, "I'm really sorry I killed your dad." And what that meant to me was his awareness that he'd actually killed a wonderful human being.'

From this meeting a remarkable partnership grew between Jo Berry and Patrick Magee. For over twenty years they have appeared together at many meetings and on discussion forums as a means of promoting the ideals of peace and reconciliation. 'I decided to go ahead and go public because I thought with the peace process still in the very early stages, if this can bring more peace to Northern Ireland then it's worth it,' she said. 'If it means fewer people are going to be hurt. You can't change the past. Nothing is going to bring my dad back, or the others – so it's about creating a different future for my children and their children.' In October 2009, the twenty-fifth anniversary of the Brighton Bombing, they chose Brighton as the place to launch their charity, Building Bridges for Peace, which is dedicated to healing divided communities and promoting better understanding of the roots of conflict.

At one point, as we talked, Jo broke off and looked around in amazement. 'I can't believe we're here,' she said. I was no less amazed to hear her story. I knew, of course, about Jo's contact with her father's killer in the name of peace and reconciliation. And I'm afraid I originally believed it to be wrong-headed, naive even. But time has passed, bitterness subsides. And Jo's integrity, her commitment to healing, shone through when we met. It is not just Jo who has gone on a journey but others, like me, who did not have her fortitude or vision. When I told her I now completely understood, and admired, her path and achievements she replied that this was 'moving' to hear. 'If my dad was here he'd say he understood, and be proud of me,' she said. I have no doubt that's true.

When I left the Grand Hotel that afternoon I looked back at its splendidly restored façade, with not a crack in it to indicate the terrible blow it suffered in 1984, and reflected on the morning I had stood there contemplating the gaping hole, and the horror and misery it betokened. And then I turned away along the seafront – still feeling sad and angry, but also uplifted for having met Jo Berry again.

Illustration Credits

SECOND PLATE SECTION

PAGE ONE: top: Royal Pavilion & Museums, Brighton & Hove; bottom: Southern Water

PAGE TWO: Wiltshire Museum & Archive

PAGE THREE: top: Ordnance Survey; middle left: public domain; middle right: courtesy of John Allen; bottom: Crown Copyright

PAGE FOUR: top: courtesy of Paul Stokes, graphics by Drakelow Tunnels; bottom far left: courtesy of Natasha Walter; bottom left: courtesy of Michael Barton

PAGE FIVE: top: National Archives and Records Administration (NARA); bottom: Transparent TV

PAGE SIX: top: Crown copyright © 1957; bottom: courtesy of Peter West

PAGE SEVEN: top: courtesy of Mark Nicholson; middle: courtesy of Paul Berriff; bottom: courtesy of Karen Grimaldi

PAGE EIGHT: top: Royal Pavilion & Museums, Brighton & Hove; bottom: *The Argus Archive* / Brighton & Hove Stuff

Index